TERRY

TERRY

MY DAUGHTER'S LIFE-AND-DEATH

STRUGGLE WITH ALCOHOLISM

George McGovern

VILLARD NEW YORK

For Terry and her treasures,
Marian and Colleen—
for Eleanor, her best friend—
and for Ann, Sue, Steve, and Mary,
who loved her.

They shall not
grow old, as we
that are left
grow old:

Age shall not weary
them, nor the years
condemn.

At the going down
of the sun and in the morning

We will remember
them.

—Laurence Binyon, 1914

Terry, age twenty-two, at her favorite lake near Charlottesville, Virginia.

PREFACE

"TERRY" WAS WHAT everyone called her. When she was born, we named her Teresa Jane McGovern. She came to prefer being called by her proper name, Teresa, but somehow, almost from the beginning, Terry seemed the perfect name for this engaging, fun-loving, pretty little girl.

I had a special name for her: "the Bear." Over the years, putting an arm around her shoulder, I would proclaim, "The ol' Bear," or "Ter' the Bear." How this affectionate term originated I've forgotten, but perhaps it was because as a toddler she reminded me of a playful cub.

Early on, she developed a habit of pulling a tiny piece of fuzz from a teddy bear, or a doll, or a shaggy blanket, and rolling it between her fingers or gently across her upper lip. This was the way she went to sleep as a child—and it continued to the end.

June 10, 1949, was a sweltering hot day in Mitchell, South Dakota, as my wife, Eleanor, gave birth to Teresa Jane, our third daughter. Eleanor recalls that delivery as the easiest of our five children, but I still remember fashioning a fan from a newspaper in the stifling maternity ward and trying to cool the perspiring young mother.

Forty-five years later, on December 12, 1994, Madison, Wisconsin, was covered with seven inches of snow and the temperature was far below freezing. Teresa left a Madison bar that night, stumbled into the snow, and froze to death.

She had fallen before from excessive drinking in every season of the year. But this time, there was too much snow, too much cold, for a fragile body to overcome. How could this have happened? My lovable little girl who had given me ten thousand laughs, countless moments of affection and joy, and, yes, years of anxiety and disappointment—now frozen to death like some deserted outcast? Terry had a multitude of friends who admired and loved her everywhere she had ever lived, gone to school, worked, or played. They all testify to her kindness, her warmth, her intelligence, her compassion, her marvelous wit. Why then did she drink so much and die so young?

The blunt answer is that Teresa Jane McGovern was an alcoholic—one of twenty million alcoholics in the United States. She died as over 100,000 other American alcoholics do every year. The difference with Terry was that she was the daughter of a prominent family. She had campaigned across the country in 1972 for her dad, the Democratic nominee for President. The moment her body was identified, her death was news around the world.

Every day, three hundred Americans die quietly of alcoholism. Many of them go unnoticed. Some of them have been out of touch with their families for years. There might be a small news item reporting that the police have found an unidentified body in a park or on the street or in a cheap rooming house—or in a snowbank. These people are usually not the subject of public notice or concern. But each one of them is a precious soul who was once a little girl or boy filled with promise and dreams. They are the silent victims of the nation's number one health problem—alcoholism. They just didn't happen to come from a prominent family, so nobody notices when they die.

In Terry's case, I could not have escaped, even if I had tried, the avalanche of reporters' questions. Immediately, I decided to respond openly and candidly about her life and death.

Yes, she died while intoxicated. Yes, she was an alcoholic—and had been for much of her life. Yes, we were aware of this and were in communication with her until the last hours of her life. Yes, she was in and out of treatment many times. Yes, she had periods of sobriety during which she fell in love and gave birth to two delightful daughters, Marian and Colleen. Yes, she fought her addiction to alcohol until the day she died.

There were other questions I could not answer then and still find it difficult to answer. Why do some people recover from alcoholism while my daughter died despite all her struggles to overcome her addiction? Why did my daughter become addicted at all?

I was open about Terry's death not only because it was virtually impossible to be silent about it, but because I wanted both her life and her death to be understood and appreciated—and I wanted others to gain from the lessons her life can teach us.

I write this book for the same reason. I want my fellow citizens and especially my fellow parents to know that alcoholism is a deadly disease that can strike any family—rich or poor, wise or foolish, strong or weak, young or old. Alcoholism is like a thief in the night. It can steal up on you and seize your life, liberty, and pursuit of happiness before you comprehend what has happened.

Most people can take a drink or two with no serious consequences. Not so the alcoholic, who is powerless to stop drinking once the addiction takes control. Alcoholism will ruin your life and kill you as surely as a raging cancer if it is not properly treated and contained.

Terry came to understand all of this. And yet she repeatedly relapsed from hard-gained sobriety into more bouts of uncontrolled drinking. In the end, her struggle to recover failed.

I believe, however, that in some respects, she speaks more powerfully in death than she was able to do in life. Both her life and her death have taught me much. Perhaps most significantly she has taught me that life is not only precious, it is fragile and uncertain—and that we need to love each other more. I wish that I had held her closer as she was and judged her less by what I wanted her to be. I wish that I had always separated my resentment of her disease and its behavior from my love for her. My father was fond of the old admonition "Hate the sin but love the sinner." I would add: "Hate the alcoholism—but love the victim."

Terry's death has given me the wisdom and the inspiration to cherish more those who survive, however perilously. I believe her story has much to inspire and enrich us: her lifetime battle with alcoholism, her remarkable insights into the meaning and travails of life and death, her compassion for all living creatures, her humor and philosophy, her tragic mistakes and suffering.

She could always warm my soul or make me laugh or break my heart. Now her body is at rest in Washington's Rock Creek Cemetery in the shadow of a Celtic cross overlooking the nation's capital, where she spent so much of her life. But her spirit is more real and present to me than at any previous time in her short and troubled life.

Since this is my personal story of Terry, I must tell you that the loss of a child—no matter the age, five, twenty-five, or forty-five—produces more grief than you can imagine. And the longer that child has lived, the more memories, associations, and shared history flood your heart and mind. We parents, after all, create our children and are given the glorious opportunity to nurture them. In a sense we see them as an extension of ourselves. When your child develops serious troubles and then dies, no amount of assurance from friends that you were not responsible for the outcome is entirely persuasive. You're going to suffer a thousand regrets and seizures of grief no matter how many times you intellectually agree that it is not your fault.

Terry was dealt a doubly cruel hand: the companion demons depression and alcoholism. They were demons that warred ceaselessly against the other aspects of her being—a warm and sunny disposition, a quick wit to make you smile or laugh, a frank and open candor that disarmed you and pricked your pomp and hypocrisy, a keen mind with a sensitivity to literature, art, and poetry, an amazing insight into and concern about the problems of others, a hunger for spiritual meaning, a love of animals, birds, and flowers, and a devotion to her family and friends.

She had all of this and more, but after her teenage years the demons were always after her, relentlessly pulling at her stability and happiness. They took turns battering her with sadness and despair, which no doctor or medication seemed able to resolve, and with alcoholic bouts, which she seemed powerless to contain very long. Yet, she persisted through countless AA meetings, numerous treatment facilities, hospitals, detox centers, and spiritual quests, and a thousand counseling sessions. No victim in my acquaintance of either alcoholism or depression ever fought harder or more courageously to overcome these related diseases than did Terry. But in the end, the demons won the physical battle and dragged her battered body to an untimely grave.

The life and death of this valiant young woman have taught me more than I could ever have imagined, not only about alcoholism and depression, but about love and life and family and, yes, about loss and death and grief.

This book has been a difficult pursuit for me. In the years since graduate school at Northwestern I have done most of my serious writing early in the morning. But this effort to tell Terry's story has been done mostly during the long nights since her death. I have written every word in longhand on pads of yellow legal-size paper. Those sheets show many small smudges. That is what happens when tears fall onto the page.

But writing this book has also been a healing experience. I wrote it to come to terms with Terry and myself. I do not know much about those who believe that we can communicate with the dead. But writing this book has given me a new appreciation, admiration, and love for dear Terry. Terry's death and my quest to understand her life have also deepened my love for my other daughters, my son, my wife, my wondrous grandchildren, and my fellow human beings.

It is my hope that Terry's life-and-death struggle with alcoholism as related here will help in some way to open the eyes, instruct the minds, and warm the hearts of other strugglers along the way.

It is those bittersweet related experiences that compose the story that I tell you in this book that begins with a little girl called Terry.

TERRY

Terry, age eleven, at the piano.

ONE

"Who can hurt me when I'm frozen?"

S HORTLY BEFORE 11:30 P.M., December 13, 1994, the doorbell rang at our home in Northwest Washington. We live
in a quiet, secluded neighborhood known as Forest Hills that ad-
joins Rock Creek Park. It is unusual for anyone to ring a doorbell at this hour; not expecting visitors, I was startled.

On this Tuesday night, Eleanor and I had enjoyed a pleasant
evening at Otello's Restaurant just below Dupont Circle—about
ten minutes from our home. The owner, who sometimes dou-
bles at the piano for the entertainment of his patrons, had played
a couple of request numbers for us—the old Beatles song "Hey
Jude" and some selections from *My Fair Lady*. I was still humming
these tunes when we arrived home.

Eleanor had gone upstairs and was in bed reading a novel.
After playing the piano for a few minutes, I had gone into our
second-floor living room, lit a small log in our fireplace, and
begun scanning the current issue of *Harper's* magazine. Puzzling
over the late-night ringing of the doorbell, I went downstairs to
see who might be there. As I descended the last steps of the open
stairway I could see two men through the glass on each side of

the large front door. One appeared to be a police officer, the other a clergyman. My heart sank. Their grave, official appearance did not portend welcome news.

"Senator McGovern, we're sorry to come to your home so late," said the officer, "but we have some sad news we must relate to you. Your daughter, Teresa Jane McGovern, was found dead today in Madison, Wisconsin, apparently frozen in the snow while intoxicated."

"Oh no!" I cried.

Then I simply went numb. I could not weep, or think, or speak.

"The Dane County coroner in Madison has asked us to tell you that he is standing by and wishes you to call him no matter how late the hour," the officer said. "We're sorry to bring you such bad news."

Trying to console me, the clergyman placed a hand on my shoulder and said a few comforting words. I thanked the two men for their kindness and then walked into my darkened den and began pacing slowly around the room. Aware there was nothing more they could do, the men quietly left.

As soon as I could manage to speak, I telephoned the coroner in Madison, Ray Wosepka. He knew the Wisconsin members of my family—my daughter Susan and her husband, Jim Rowen, formerly of Madison and in recent years residents of Milwaukee, where Jim works at the *Milwaukee Journal-Sentinel* and Susan at the University of Wisconsin. The coroner also knew Teresa well enough to know that she had suffered from a longtime drinking problem. He gave me the few details available about her death and explained that he would have more information after an autopsy had been performed the next day. I was incapable of asking more than a few faltering questions, so I thanked the coroner for his thoughtfulness, hung up, and began pacing again.

And then it dawned on me: I must go upstairs and tell Eleanor that our troubled daughter, whom she had loved, nurtured, and laughed and cried with for so many years, was now gone—frozen in the December snows of Wisconsin. How could I possibly announce to dear Eleanor anything so utterly devastating? Could she withstand the shock?

I stalled for perhaps fifteen minutes before informing Eleanor of Terry's death, first because it was such a painful task, and second because I harbored a desperate hope that the coroner might call and tell me that they had revived Terry, or that they had made a mistake in identifying the body. But finally I trudged up the stairs to our third-floor bedroom. Eleanor was sleeping soundly—her reading lamp still lighted, her book fallen to the floor. As I looked at the lovely, gentle face on the pillow, I began to weep convulsively.

Gathering Eleanor in my arms as she awakened, I blurted out, "This is the saddest news I will ever tell you. Terry is gone. She died today in Madison, apparently after heavy drinking and a collapse in the snow." Eleanor's response was a cry heartrending and terrible. I can neither describe nor forget it.

"Oh God, oh God, what happened? What happened? No, no, no, no, no." All I could do was to hold her tightly and weep with her. It was the saddest moment of our more than fifty years of marriage.

As I tried to console Eleanor, I was seized by a searing pain that made me move away. Terry, the delightful but afflicted daughter I had been especially close to from the beginning, was dead. How could this be? How could this endearing child have drifted so far over the years that she ended up dying alone in the snow?

Pacing the floor, agonizing over these questions, I began to think of my other children. They must be told of Terry's death.

It was shortly after midnight when I called our oldest daughter, Ann, a teacher in Riverdale, Maryland, and broke the news to her. Ann had expressed alarm for the past two years about Terry's deepening alcoholism. She and her husband, Frank Wilson, had even driven to Wisconsin in the spring of 1993 to be with Terry for a few days in what they feared might be her last months of life. Ann was stunned and grief-stricken to have her fears verified, but I sensed that it was in some way a confirmation rather than a total shock. She and her family arrived about two in the morning—it was then December 14—to be with us for the rest of the night. Meanwhile, I telephoned our second daughter, Susan, in Milwaukee. She had been with Terry frequently in recent years and had believed for a while that by showing her love for her sister, she could somehow redeem her from alcoholism. Terry had first moved to Wisconsin in 1976 when Susan invited her to come and live with her and her husband and their two young sons, Matthew and Sam. The death of her younger sister sent Sue into a deep grief that has continued.

Our youngest daughter, Mary, was expecting to give birth to a second child in a few months, so I did not telephone her until early the next morning. As a rising United Nations professional, she had been out of the country or working in New York City over the past decade and was not as close to Terry as Susan and Ann. She also carried a measure of both personal and occupational stress that had prompted her to avoid becoming too enmeshed in Terry's struggles.

Steve, Terry's only brother, who is three years her junior, was not reachable by telephone during the night. Ann and her son Tim told him of Terry's death the next morning. Stunned, he left a friend's apartment and walked slowly down Connecticut Avenue. "Curiously," he later said, "a kind of calming relief came over me as I thought, 'Finally, Terry is at peace.' I found myself smiling through the tears."

DURING THE LAST two weeks of the previous June, our family, including Teresa and her two little girls, Marian, nine, and Colleen, seven, had gathered for a vacation in a big house on North Carolina's Outer Banks. Ann and Susan were there with their husbands and five sons, along with Eleanor and me. Terry, an accomplished swimmer, loved the ocean. We all enjoyed the sun, surf, and saltwater spray on the vast beaches of the Atlantic, although Terry struggled at times against her craving for alcohol. She could not always hide her pain; her normal enthusiasm and cheerfulness were somewhat subdued during these days.

Terry's brother-in-law, Jim Rowen, recalls a moment when he and Terry found themselves relaxing on the sand while the children splashed in the ocean. Aware of the tension that sometimes existed in the family because of her drinking, Terry tried to break the ice by asking Jim how he thought the Milwaukee Brewers baseball team would fare that season. "She knew I was a baseball nut, but I knew she didn't give a damn about professional sports, yet she wanted to embrace me conversationally by coming over on my ground," Jim noted.

When asked to recall pleasurable moments with their mother, Marian and Colleen talked excitedly about Terry's twice taking them to a popular carnival on the Outer Banks complete with rides on the roller coaster. They remember Terry's smiling face as she waved to them on their rides, obviously relishing their fun. But they also recall their mother's embarrassment and apology when they discovered that she had downed a large bottle of ale.

Terry lived with this kind of dichotomy for most of her life: a fun-loving, humorous, engaging personality who brought joy to her family and friends—but also, at times, the clouds of alcoholism and depression.

Her wit and infectious laughter have been noted by every one of her friends I have interviewed. Dawn Newsome, who knew her intimately over many years, tells of Terry's "earthy" sense of humor, which she witnessed on a shopping mission when Terry was interested in buying a pair of Timberland boots. "Why are they so much more expensive than the other brands? Are they worth the difference?" Terry asked the clerk. Very seriously, the clerk inquired, "Do you really want me to give you all the facts?" "Naw," said Terry, "just give me a crock of shit." The somber clerk burst out laughing.

"I can't recall once when Terry failed to come up with a quip when she needed a retort to bring down the barriers," Dawn told me. "No matter how young or old, mighty or humble, Terry sooner or later would have people laughing, or at least feeling better."

There are times in the alcoholic's life, however, when humor fails—seemingly every cell in the body screams in real pain for alcohol. Those terrible times were never far from closing in on Terry. The nonalcoholic cannot grasp the genuine anguish involved. Terry did not escape that distress on the Outer Banks, but largely she resisted it with a supreme effort to protect the pleasure of the rest of us. That was the last time we saw her alive.

Following that family vacation, Eleanor and I took off for the University of Innsbruck, Austria, where I was a guest lecturer for the next six weeks. Terry returned to Madison with her daughters. We had very little contact with her during the summer and early fall. Indeed, we had decided—with the encouragement of a counselor—that it might be best for both Terry and for us not to be deeply involved for a time.

In mid-November, Eleanor and I left Washington on a business trip to the Persian Gulf, ending with a few days in Italy and a Thanksgiving dinner at the lovely mountain seaside home of our friend Gore Vidal. Just before that trip, Eleanor received a letter from Terry postmarked November 4 in which she wrote:

> *I truly cannot believe I've let myself stay sick for so long. It's been 4 years relapsing—pulling my life apart and damaging the spirits of those I love most. I wonder if I can ever really have a full life knowing my children and I have lost precious time and not knowing what time I will be allowed now. I'm so sad mom. Please pray for Marian, Colleen and me to be reunited. I want to be a daughter to you and dad—not a source of worry, anger and sorrow. I want to be a sister to my brother and sisters. I've played around with my recovery—somehow unable to grasp how serious it is; how much suffering it has caused me and others.*

We had only a few brief telephone conversations with Terry during the next few weeks, hoping that our maintaining a certain distance might prompt her to confront her alcohol dependence. But her drinking problem steadily worsened during this period from mid-July to mid-December.

There has not been a day since Terry's death that I have not anguished over our decision. I regret every phone call not made, every letter not written, every missed opportunity to be with her and to share her pain.

FROM OCTOBER 1980 until the summer of 1988, Terry maintained the longest period of sobriety in her adult life. It was during this period that she met and fell in love with Raymond Frey, a Wisconsin social worker. Although they never married, they lived together for several years and became excellent parents to two daughters, Marian, born in 1985, and Colleen, born in 1987. They faced the usual strains and pressures of trying to rear children and maintain a home on a limited income, but they also developed clashing emotional needs that made it difficult to sustain their relationship. Terry, a recovering alcoholic, was also a sensitive and loving person who desperately needed the emotional support of an affectionate and caring mate. Ray was caught up, as are so many young fathers, in making a living. He perhaps needed more personal distance than Terry could tolerate. After five years of living together, they came to a mutual agreement that Ray should leave, at least for a trial period. Terry believed that after a few weeks of separation, Ray would miss her as much as she did him, and would return as a more understanding and loving mate. But this was not to be.

Ray had scarcely departed in mid-October 1988 before Terry went into a painful time of alternating regret, jealousy, resentment, sorrow, anger, and self-pity, culminating in her relapse into drinking. She lacked the personal resources to care for two energetic, demanding little girls by herself; nor could she escape the sense of rejection she felt because Ray had begun a new relationship with a woman who had also been Terry's friend.

When an alcoholic relapses after a lengthy sobriety, recovery is extremely difficult. The disease continues its insidious course even in sobriety and grips the victim with new force when a relapse occurs. To her credit, Terry recognized the seriousness of her resumed drinking and placed herself in a long-term recovery program in Milwaukee. A young mother invariably finds such a program especially painful and difficult because it separates her from her dependent children. But Terry succeeded over the next year with a determined effort.

Four days into this experience at Recovery House, she wrote in her journal on October 29, 1989:

Sitting here in my room, feeling the old, familiar gnawing emptiness, I know I must continue with my meditation. It is the most valuable time I have. . . . I listen to the wind. I wish I were in my new home listening to this wind while my babies sleep.

But at the end of the day, she knew that she must remain in Milwaukee struggling with her recovery:

11:15 p.m. The day is over and I'm going to bed with a good feeling. What I learned today that will help me stay sober are some of the things that caused my relapse:
   1. *I didn't want to give up drinking completely—*
   2. *Dishonest—if I had been honest I would have thought through the consequences. I didn't because I was in DENIAL.*
   3. *Tried to do it alone—thought therapy and self knowledge were my best tools—*
   4. *Didn't develop my spiritual life*
   5. *Stopped going to meetings [AA]*
   6. *Stopped using a sponsor.*

Here I will learn the attitudes and thought patterns that lead to unhappiness and then using.

This energetic, full-time recovery program meant that for the first time Ray was the primary caretaker of four-year-old Marian and two-year-old Colleen. He cooperated in driving the children from Madison to Milwaukee for a visit each weekend. Terry's treatment continued for much of 1990 as she received outpatient care while living in her own apartment in Milwaukee. All went well until she decided to move back to Madison to be with her children. Then the same old anxieties, stresses, and depression returned, and she sought relief in her old friend alcohol. She made other serious efforts in recovery programs in Wisconsin, Washington, D.C., and Maryland—but each in turn was soon followed by a relapse.

During the last four years of her life—beginning March 25, 1991, and ending December 12, 1994—she was admitted to the Tellurian Detox Center in Madison sixty-eight times—usually after collapsing and sometimes injuring herself while heavily intoxicated. On one occasion, she fell facedown in a pool of water and nearly drowned. Several times she suffered painful head or facial abrasions from falling on the sidewalks or streets of Madison. At other times, she passed out on a bus, on a park bench, or in a store and was then taken to the detox center or a nearby hospital after someone called 911. She became a familiar, forlorn figure to the Madison police, emergency crews, and hospitals and the ever-beckoning detox center.

These many detoxifications kept Terry alive, but they were miserable experiences. One veteran of such places describes it this way: "Imagine yourself withdrawing from alcohol in a detox ward. You may be racked with tremors so severe you can't lift a cup of coffee. Your stomach feels like it wants to leap up your throat. Every muscle in your body aches. You can hardly walk to the bathroom."

Laura Blumenfeld, a *Washington Post* reporter who wrote of Terry's death in the Sunday, February 5, 1995, issue, has captured some of the conditions Terry lived with as she moved in and out of the Tellurian Detox Center in her last months:

> As the months passed, her stomach swelled, the veins in her esophagus dilated, and she was throwing up blood. . . . In the spitting, cursing, dark halls of detox, where alarms blare if patients break the laser beams across their doors, where the cinder-block walls are covered with squares of foam so patients don't crack their heads, Terry was something of an oddity. She believed she would get well. She was sweet and articulate. She read books and used Estée Lauder blush.
>
> There was another difference with Terry. She was one of the only patients who still had people on the outside who cared. Her father was always sending her roses. When the roses withered, she wound them around her headband, smiling: "They love me, they do."

Even at the detox center, while her body jittered from with-drawal, she would limp out of bed to soothe her roommate, or pad down the hall in a robe to bring her orange juice. In group therapy she liked to comfort others, rather than focus on her own troubles.

Her warmth helped heal other alcoholics even if she couldn't heal herself. One friend from detox, a man named Don, tells of the time he escaped from a treatment facility with a lunatic plan to run away to Bangkok. He called Terry from the platform at the Amtrak station. She had precisely fifteen minutes to persuade him to come back to the facility.

Later, they celebrated his sobriety by spray-painting his ini-tials on a rock along with his recovery date, 12/25/89. Christ-mas. Then Don sprayed TJM. Teresa Jane McGovern. He asked her, "What's the anniversary of your recovery?"

She smiled crookedly and said: "Just put a question mark."

In early 1993, in an effort to break this increasingly sad and dangerous pattern, Eleanor and I persuaded Terry to enter a special treatment program at the National Institutes of Health in Bethesda, Maryland. She cooperated, as did Eleanor and I, with the six-week treatment agenda, which included counseling and group-discussion sessions with family members of other pa-tients. We were encouraged by Terry's serious effort, hopeful at-titude, and apparent progress into recovery.

On the morning of her completion of the program, I drove to the NIH center and brought her to our Washington home. She asked if she could use my car for a few minutes to pick up a prescription at a nearby drugstore. Three hours later I was called by a concerned bartender who informed me that Terry had collapsed from heavy drinking. It pains me even now to re-call the sad and bitter disappointment, the personal regret and doubt about my own judgment, that followed. And let me be frank about this. I was furious. How many times should we arrange these treatment programs for her? How many thousands of dollars should we invest in failing efforts to assist her recovery? What about the resentment of our other children, who felt that their parents were obsessed with Terry?

"I guess the best way to get attention in this family is to be an alcoholic," Ann once told me.

Were we helping Terry, or enabling her to put off facing her addiction and coming to grips with it? Perhaps indirectly we were contributing to an illness that, if not confronted, could claim her life.

"Dad, I don't think Terry will ever get well as long as you and Mom keep bailing her out," my daughter Susan told me with a mixture of disgust and anguish.

A few months later, while having lunch with Michael Deaver, a longtime aide to President Reagan, I mentioned my deep concern over Terry's drinking problem. He immediately arranged for her to go through one of the most highly regarded treatment centers in the nation—Father Martin's Ashley House at Havre de Grace, Maryland. Michael drove her there himself that same night, after picking her up at Georgetown University Hospital.

After six weeks of a specialized program designed to prepare patients against the danger of future relapses, Terry was urged to live for the next six months or more in the supportive environment of a halfway house with other recovering alcoholics. She, however, was desperate to return to Madison to be with her daughters, so she rejected this advice, as she had on earlier occasions. Eleanor agreed to accompany her to Madison and remain until she could find an apartment and a job. With her usual patience and love, Eleanor stayed with her for two weeks, but the day she left, Terry started drinking again.

"How can you keep doing this to yourself and to your family?" I asked.

"I don't know, Dad," she said wearily. "I guess I'm just an alcoholic."

And yet, never once did Terry give up the struggle to move from relapses back to sobriety. With her body crying out in pain for alcohol, her spirit longed for sobriety. Physically she got high temporarily on alcohol and then crashed into despair again. But the high her heart and mind craved was simply to feel stable and secure. All the evidence and the testimony of her closest friends leave no doubt that Terry tried until the end to resist the powerful claims of her body against her spiritual longing for a sober, satisfying life. Her sister Susan has noted that Terry's journals tell of a valiant and perceptive nurturing of her soul even while her body was falling victim to alcoholism.

Her diary of 1993 carries these poignant notations: "August 25: Last Drink. August 26: First day sober"—with a colorful X. Each day thereafter is highlighted by a Magic Marker X indicating a day of sobriety until September 14, when the notation reads, "Relapse"—with no X. The next day, September 15, she simply notes, "crying"—but with an X indicating she stayed sober despite her misery. The "crying" appears again the next day with another sobriety X. Two more X's appear on September 17 and 18, and then no more—nineteen days of sobriety, a one-day relapse, four more days of painful sobriety, and then a relapse. This was the pattern of much of the last four years of her life, except for longer periods of abstinence when she was confined for treatment, and increasingly shorter times of nondrinking and more frequent relapses when she was not confined.

AS I HAVE pursued the course of Terry's life since her death and pulled my own recollections into at least some degree of coherence, I am convinced that she was haunted by a growing

sense of abandonment, a loss of self-esteem, and a painful, recurring depression. Those feelings were strongly fed by the departure of Ray. They were also aggravated by the ending of
subsequent relationships, including one of special significance
a year before her own death. A young male friend and sometimes
drinking partner of Terry's named Steve, whom she cared for
deeply and whose companionship she treasured, died alone, intoxicated, in the snow only a couple of blocks from Terry's even-
tual place of death. Terry brooded constantly over this loss,
which led to many hours of sorrow, regret, and loneliness. She
and Steve had talked about working together on their recovery
and then marrying. She had once asked Eleanor and me to accompany her to the place of Steve's death, where we each placed
a flower as she said yet another farewell to her fallen friend. The
pattern of her death so closely duplicated Steve's that it is possible his death provided a blueprint for her own.

On July 29, 1990, ten months after her separation from Ray,
this notation appears in her journal:

*Abandonment—I feel it—it hurts. No one to make me feel safe, protected.
I cry. . . . I have looked so long for someone to protect me, love me without anger or shame. I feel anxious, hold my breath. If someone looks too
closely, I freeze like a chameleon—ready to change color (identity) to
protect myself. Better to freeze*
—who can hurt me when I'm frozen?

Behind the sense of abandonment and loss of self-esteem was
the ever-lurking alcoholism that frequently separated her from
friends, recreation, romance, social acceptance, and even the
treasures of her life—her two little daughters. When Ray was
given primary custody of her children, a vital part of her reason
for being died. She sought constantly to offset these losses by

telephone calls and socializing with a wide circle of friends who loved her and delighted in her company—when she was sober; they were never quite certain when alcohol might interrupt the relationship. She spent many long days and nights alone, except for a kitten, parakeet, dog, turtle, or some other pet, sometimes in apartments that she would rent for a while and then lose, or in the spare bedroom of a friend's home.

She treasured her shabby, secondhand furniture, her pictures and other wall hangings, her jewelry, her carefully preserved journals, photo albums, letters, and gifts, and the drawings and papers her children brought home from school. Each time she lost an apartment, she would carefully load all of her things into a small truck—sometimes borrowed from a friend—and place everything back in storage. No matter how ill she became, no matter how discouraged with her life, she clung to these personal treasures to the end. It has astounded me, as I have gone through her possessions, to discover how this desperately ill daughter preserved everything, going back in some cases to the early years of her life. I think she must have protected every little trinket ever given to her.

Separated from her possessions as she frequently was, she felt deserted and homeless. Her medication of choice for these sad times was alcohol. As her brain cells were more and more impaired with alcohol, she was increasingly unable to control either her intake or her decision-making capability. In the last year of her life, she told her sister Ann, "My body no longer recognizes any food other than alcohol." Its ravages steadily made everything in her life worse. But as the disease progressed, she tried to protect us from anxiety by withholding information about her deepening illness.

I fear that we unwittingly added to her sense of abandonment by following the advice to distance ourselves in the last months of her life when she may have most needed to feel our love and presence. She called a friend, Don Berlin, collect from a pay phone, having just been released from the detox center shortly after Thanksgiving—two weeks before her death. Eleanor and I were traveling in the Middle East, and Terry was aware that we had stepped back somewhat from involvement with her. She also tended to hold me responsible for the "distancing" in the last months of her life. "I understand why they are doing it," she told Don, "but I feel bad about it. I only wish that my dad knew how much I love him."

I wish I could tell her: "Dear Terry, I hope you know how much I love you. And I wish I had told you that more when you were alive and struggling with the demon that controlled your brain." I try not to berate myself for the things that I cannot now correct, but if I had those months to live over again . . .

Well, I will tell you what I would do with a second chance: I would never forget that alcoholism is a disease, that I should hate the disease but care for its victim—just as I would react if a loved one were suffering from cancer or diabetes. I tried to maintain these attitudes with Terry, but frequently my anger at her behavior in the grip of alcoholism translated into resentment and disappointment directed at her instead of her illness.

Sometimes when I called her I would begin: "Who's ahead today—you or the demon?" She loved that way of posing the problem. It was a clear indication that I was separating the demon that I hated from the precious victim whom I loved.

But there should have been more of this understanding, and it should have been given more force and consistency. Terry, as a desperately ill human being suffering from alcoholism, should not have been left to walk and fall in the streets, to be evicted from her apartments, to drink herself into a state of blackout and collapse in public bars, to be exploited sexually and abused by strangers when she was intoxicated. She needed the unbroken love, support, and protection of her family, her friends, her neighborhood, and her community.

I ask God and I ask dear Terry to forgive me for not always faithfully adhering to these simple concerns as a father and as a member of the human family. There is no such thing as too much compassion, understanding, support, and love for the sick and dying. Alcoholics are sick unto death. They won't make it through the night without our love and protection—and sometimes our repeated direct intervention.

It is not easy to live with alcoholics, but it is far harder to live without them when death steals them away. I do not regret one single act of kindness, patience, or support that I gave to Terry. What I regret is her slowly developing death and the feeling that I could have done more to prevent it.

Nor can I escape regret over the ways in which my political career and personal ego demands deprived Terry and my other children of time, attention, direction—and fun with their father. This was a loss to me as much as to them. Almost from the beginning, there was a special relationship between Terry and me. After dubbing her "the Bear," sometimes I would attach her teddy bear to a string on the light over her bed and would awaken her for school by tapping lightly on her nose. She would smile sleepily and open her eyes knowing my trademark wake-up call.

We thrived on a shared sense of humor, a penchant for kidding, a sense of the ridiculous. She treasured that relationship, and, as the middle child separated by several years in age from her two older sisters and her younger brother and sister, she needed it.

It is sad for me to read passages in her personal journal describing the hurt and sense of loss she experienced as her dad became more and more caught up in public concerns and his personal gratification while having less and less time for her private needs. My other children have, I suppose, made similar notations. Daughters especially need a responsive and caring relationship with their fathers during adolescence. I am only comforted by the knowledge that in the fifteen years since I left the U.S. Senate, I have enjoyed much more time of close association with my children and grandchildren.

ON OCTOBER 1, 1993, I invited Terry to accompany me to Norfolk, Virginia, for a reunion of the pilots and crew members of the 455th Bomb Group, with whom I flew as a B-24 bomber pilot in World War II. She enjoyed chatting with the veteran pilots, whom she plied with questions about a chapter in her dad's life that unfolded before she was born. In her journal notes of that trip, she wrote:

> *Arrived in Norfolk for Dad's Army Air Corps reunion. Our drive down [from Washington] was easy and enjoyable. He is much easier to be with than when he was in national politics. I was going to say he had no business being so self-centered and obsessed when he had dependent children—then I thought, I have done the same thing with alcoholism. There is no difference. I will tell him sometime.*

That was her view, and it contains some truth, although some of her observations were distorted by self-pity and some were influenced by counselors who seemed not always grounded in reality. For years, Terry engaged in desperate searches for the cause of her troubled life—chemical dependence, depression, declining self-esteem. Sometimes these introspective quests were carried to pathetic rationalizations of the origins of her problems. Alcoholics have a tendency to engage in what the professionals call "externalizing"—blaming their problems on other people, including those persons they love the most.

Our family and Terry's closest friends are unanimous in believing that she was an essentially happy person in her childhood and adolescent years until her late teens. But as she sought to find an explanation for her later grief brought on by alcoholism and other chemical dependency, she tended to construct in her mind an exaggerated image of an unhappy childhood and an insensitive family.

I several times responded to her contentions of family neglect by saying, in effect, "Terry, let's assume you are right about all of this, that Eleanor and I were not always as wise as we should have been as parents. We doubtless did make mistakes, as did your sisters. But this is now history, and we can't change the past. What we can do, and what you can do, is to move on from those mistakes we cannot change to facing as best we can the problems and responsibilities of today." I think such reality challenges made her uncomfortable because she was in fact living in pain, uncertainty, and anxiety caused primarily by long years of alcoholism. It was indeed painful to accept responsibility for her own life—including her own past mistakes—and she had to find some deeper explanation for the alcoholism that caused it all.

Donald Rogers, Chandler Scott McMillan, and Morris Hill are part of a growing consensus among the nation's top alcoholism experts who believe that almost without exception, the emotional problems of an alcoholic are caused by alcoholism rather than the emotional problems causing the alcoholism. They write that "far from drinking to 'cover up' or self-medicate an underlying mental or emotional disturbance, the alcoholic experiences depressions, mood swings, personality problems, and general 'craziness' because of alcoholism and the experience of alcoholic drinking. There is strong evidence, obtained from studies that span decades in the lives of their subjects, that alcoholics show no special incidence of personality or psychological disorder prior to the onset of their alcoholism."

I am now certain that alcoholism is in considerable part a physiological disease based on the victim's genetic inheritance. It is probably arrogant for me to assume, as I sometimes have, that I had the power to prevent or cure that disease in one of my children. Terry drank too much—not because of anything she or Eleanor or I did or did not do, nor because she lacked willpower. She drank too much because she was an alcoholic. Her first drinks as an early teenager seem to have been stimulated by peer pressure; her later addiction stemmed at least in part from a genetic vulnerability that accompanied her at birth. As the saying goes among alcoholics, "One drink is too much, a thousand too little."

My son, Steve, a recovering alcoholic, sheds some light on the cravings of alcoholics in an interview with Laura Blumenfeld:

"I can numb the pain," says a voice. "It doesn't sound like an evil voice. It sounds like a friend, telling you the truth."

Teresa's younger brother, Steven McGovern, is describing the voice of alcohol, as it whispers to you when you are feeling tense or dissatisfied or empty: "Here's your old pal, I can get you through this." . . .

"At first," says Steve, "it sounds like the solution to all your vague unnamed fears. Then the fog clears. And the voice is laughing at you.

" 'Gotcha again.'

"You're left standing alone, among the destruction. You realize it took twenty years of your life. You're sober, you feel itchy, shaky, your chest squeezes and it's hard to breathe. Your body is crying for it."

The night Steve heard of Terry's death, he lay in bed and smiled, and he talked to his sister:

"Well, you're free now!"

"I couldn't help feeling happy for her. We were celebrating together. We were laughing and hugging."

On December 7, one week before her death, Terry called me at 9:45 A.M. to ask if I could help her with the financing of an apartment, which I agreed to do. She then left the detox center, ending a five-day confinement, and made her way to the Marquette Elementary School in time for an 11:15 lunch with Marian. She loved brief times such as these with her daughters, who were the joys of her life. Marian and Colleen savored such visits with their mother too, but they became increasingly anxious when Terry appeared after she had been drinking.

Records at the detox center for the previous three weeks tell a story: Terry was admitted November 14 and discharged later the next day, and then readmitted the same day, discharged November 17 and readmitted the same day, discharged November 19, readmitted November 20, discharged November 22, readmitted November 23, left of her own volition November 29, readmitted December 1, left of her own volition December 2, and readmitted the same day. After being released December 7, she remained sober until after her lunch with Marian shortly before noon.

But during the afternoon the drinking resumed, and by the time she visited seven-year-old Colleen's Lapham Elementary School she was partially intoxicated. She arrived at 3:00 P.M. when Colleen was just getting on the school bus to go home. Terry joined her on the bus, quietly apologizing for her drinking. "Mommy, I wish you didn't drink, but I want to be with you whether you're drinking or not," Colleen said. Terry said good-bye to little Colleen on the porch of her home on Rutledge Street. It was the last time she was to see either of her daughters.

At eight o'clock that night, she stumbled into a familiar co-operative grocery store in her old neighborhood on Williamson Street, not only intoxicated but also wet and cold from an apparent earlier collapse in the heavy snow.

Anna Bose, a clerk in the store, where Terry had shopped over the years, noted that her late-evening visitor was shaking from the cold; she was probably suffering from frostbite and hypothermia. She was also finding it difficult to speak with any coherence. After calling 911 for an ambulance, Anna asked Terry to sit with her, comforted her, and began rubbing her hands and feet with dry towels.

"And we both cried," she wrote us. "I told her that she was doing just fine, and she responded to the contact and the kindness. She kissed me on the cheek and said, 'I know you.' And I thought—I know you and how you are struggling."

Later that night after the paramedics had taken her to St. Mary's Hospital for treatment, an orderly went into the examination room to check on her. He found her curled up in a ball under a blanket, soaking wet, shivering and frightened. It was not the first time he had encountered Terry at St. Mary's. Dropping to his knees, he asked: "Why are you doing this to yourself?"

Rocking in agony, she could only say: "I don't know. I don't know." And, indeed, she could never explain her cruel and punishing self-inflicted bouts with alcohol. Later that night, when her condition stabilized, she was taken back to the detox center, where she had been released earlier in the day.

The next afternoon, she called me at my office to ask again if I would help her secure a lease on an apartment near the house where her children lived with their father. She explained that she had saved $600 to cover the security deposit on the apartment but had lost it while drinking the night before. When I expressed my disappointment over her drinking and the loss of her money, she said: "Well, Dad, it could have been worse—I could have lost my life." I, of course, readily agreed, although I knew nothing of the close call in the snow the night before.

"Terry, your life is everything," I said. "I'll help you with the apartment, but please take care of yourself. We've sent round-trip airline tickets for you and the little girls and we're looking forward to your being home for Christmas."

She assured me that all would be well—although I detected a slight anxiety in her voice about the flight home for Christmas, a flight she knew she would be unable to make if the drinking resumed. In a call a few days earlier, she had asked me if I could determine whether her health coverage would pay for her admission to a long-term-care facility where she had once been a patient in suburban Milwaukee. What she did *not* tell me was that her counselors at the detox center had told her they were instituting steps to secure a court order that would place her involuntarily in a different long-term-care facility in Milwaukee. Although I did not know it at the time, she was terrified by this prospect and was determined to leave the detox center before such a court order could be secured and served. She had refused to sign a consent form that would have authorized her counselors to give us this information or any other information about her condition. Some months earlier, in the summer, in a telephone conversation with her counselor, I had approved the committal plan with the understanding it would be followed only if it seemed to be the only option that might save her.

Terry's first priority in her last days was to avoid involuntary long-term care. She could not bear the thought of another lengthy separation from her daughters, nor did she have much faith in the success of yet another program. That was doubtless her reason for asking me to find out if she could voluntarily return to the earlier treatment center, where she would be free to walk away to see her daughters or to reach the nearest bar. Her counselors objected to the treatment center preferred by Terry in part because one of its attractions for her was a male patient there who had in the past complicated the recovery process for her. Her alternative plan of securing an apartment was also, I now know, a strategy for avoiding the serving of a court order at the detox center. This type of scheming is typical self-destructive alcoholic behavior—maddening for caring friends, counselors, and family members. It's the product of a brain long affected by alcohol.

Shortly after Labor Day, Terry had accepted an invitation from a longtime friend, Art Lahey of nearby Horicon, Wisconsin, to stay for a while at his home, where he resided with his son. His wife, a close friend of Terry's, had died early in 1994. Terry remained sober during September and early October—even while working part-time as a waitress at a Horicon café. When her drinking resumed, Art took her back to the detox center, but stayed in frequent contact with her while she was there from October 10 until October 24, at which point she transferred to the Madison Hope Haven halfway house, where she remained until November 13. Then began the series of admissions and discharges at the detox center, which continued until her death a month later.

She was at Hope Haven on Halloween, which she wanted to be memorable for her two young daughters. She carefully worked out with them the costumes they wanted to wear: for Marian, the garb of a nun, and for Colleen, Snow White. Under Terry's instructions, Eleanor devised a child-sized nun costume and mailed it to Marian. Terry was unable to attend the Halloween party, but she proudly mailed us pictures of the girls with her at Hope Haven on the day before Halloween and other shots of the girls in their Halloween gowns.

Art had informed Terry that although it was painful for him, he had agreed to testify in court, as requested by the detox counselors, that she was unable to care for herself. Terry was dismayed. She begged him not to do so, and he finally agreed to withhold his testimony if Terry was able to stop drinking after going forward with the leasing of her apartment.

Thus fortified, she made an appointment to see her prospective landlord at the new apartment at 2:00 P.M. on Monday, December 12. Early that morning, as she had requested, I assured her landlord that I would guarantee the rent should she be unable to pay it.

Then, against the wishes of her counselor, she left the center and headed for a 10:00 A.M. appointment with an old friend, Ernie Moll. He had several years earlier helped her and her children after her separation from Raymond Frey. At one time, Ernie had even constructed a little house for the girls' pet mice. Terry had telephoned him on December 7, telling him she was worried about possible involuntary commitment to long-term treatment and asking him to help her move into an apartment. She called again on December 9 to ask if he would go to her mailbox at her apartment to see if an expected check from Eleanor was there. The check was there, and Ernie promised to hold it for her until their meeting on December 12. She arrived promptly at 10:00 A.M. on the 12th and seemed to be in high spirits.

She and Ernie spent a pleasant hour or so at his apartment, recalling good times of earlier years. Terry was excited about her new home and was pleased that her friend offered her an air mattress and a chair for temporary use and presented her with a carefully wrapped package containing her three photo albums, which he had stored for her for several years. He also agreed to build another mouse house as requested by nine-year-old Marian, provided she would help him.

Over a second cup of coffee, Ernie called a tenant in the apartment above his and arranged to borrow his pickup truck so that Terry's furniture and personal effects in storage could be moved to the new apartment on Wednesday, December 14, sometime after 5:00 P.M. "I thought this might be the attempt that works. She seemed so clear and upbeat about things," Ernie later wrote us.

Having lost her personal identification cards, including her driver's license, along with her money in the incident of December 7, Terry was worried that she would have difficulty cashing a check. Loading her albums and other personal things into his car, Ernie drove her to the Department of Motor Vehicles office to get a new driving permit, for which he provided the necessary $4. Remembering that she had lost her glasses in the earlier collapse, Ernie helped her fill out the application and then walked with her to the photo department. Always conscious of her appearance, which by her lights required modestly applied lipstick and appropriate earrings, Terry jokingly asked her friend if he had any lipstick. Even without those benefits, she proudly showed off the new instant photo, in which she wore a broad smile. In his letter to us of Thursday, December 15, Ernie wrote:

As we left the building, Terry stopped to offer assistance to an elderly man on crutches, who seemed to be having quite a struggle navigating the ice and snow at the curb. He said he was doing okay, but she took his arm anyhow to steady him as he hobbled into the building. I went ahead to the car, unlocked the doors, and got in. When she had completed her helpful task, we drove back to her apartment on Morrison Court to unload the items from the car. We were able between us to take all of the things up to the third-floor apartment in one trip. We arrived there to find two of the workmen who had done the remodeling. The floors were freshly sanded and varnished. The kitchen was all new, cupboards, appliances, and work counter, all new. A very nice apartment, with a view over the trees and rooftops toward Lake Monona. Plenty of room for the children to visit and stay over, if that was an option. Terry talked with the men about the appointment with the landlord at 2:00 p.m. They told her the place was all ready except for cleaning and carpeting in one room. They gave her a key.

I returned to the car to move it out of the driveway, where it blocked the way for other tenants. Terry came down a few minutes later. By this time it was about 12:15 p.m. Terry was confident she could go to the bank, cash the check, and return in time for the appointment. She said she had several bus passes. I assumed she would take a bus on Williamson, back to the neighborhood, and walk the few blocks over to Morrison Court. I drove to her bank across from the main library on West Main and left her there. I went to a restaurant, had lunch, and returned home.

I had expected her to call me on Tuesday or Wednesday to give me information about getting the basic items from storage. I didn't hear from her on Tuesday but was only slightly concerned. . . . On Wednesday morning, a friend called to tell me they had found her.

After cashing her check, Terry returned to the apartment in time for her 2:00 P.M. meeting with her new landlord, Bob. She had given him a $500 security deposit in November and now turned over $550 from her just-cashed check for the first month's rent.

Bob, about to observe his sixty-seventh birthday, was himself a recovering alcoholic and sympathetic to Terry. They spent the next three hours visiting and turning the pages of the photo albums that spanned her life. She told Bob of her love for her mother and father, her brother and sisters, and her little girls. She spoke excitedly about her new apartment and how wonderful it would be to have this comfortable home with a lake view located within a block of Marian and Colleen. About 5:00 P.M., as her landlord prepared to leave, she put her hands on his shoulders and said affectionately, "You know, Bob, you remind me of my father. You're very compassionate."

After agreeing to meet her landlord at the apartment again the next day at 1:00 P.M. to take care of a few minor unfinished modifications, Terry said good night, noting that she had to walk over to nearby Williamson Street to pick up a few items for the apartment. As evening approached, a damp, chilling fog crept across the city and the temperature dropped far below freezing.

Terry was warmly and neatly dressed, wearing thermal underwear, dark slacks, a heavy off-white Sandhills (N.C.) Community College pullover shirt I had given her, a red-and-black winter jacket, and a warm woolen scarf. She walked up Baldwin for three and a half blocks, crossing familiar streets where she had lived for the past seventeen years, including Rutledge, where Colleen and Marian lived with their father. I have no doubt that she walked the few paces to the left from Baldwin past the Rutledge house in the hope that she might catch a glimpse of her children through the window. She did this frequently—sometimes when she was weaving and stumbling from too much vodka. Returning to Baldwin, she would next come to Spaight, then Jenifer, where in earlier years she had rented apartments, and then her familiar neighborhood shopping street, Williamson.

When Terry entered the Crystal Corner Bar at the intersection of Williamson and Baldwin shortly after 5:00 P.M., she took a stool at the forward end of the bar near the entrance. She struck up a conversation with a veteran of the Vietnam War, who bought her a vodka on the rocks. She chatted happily with other patrons about her new apartment and ordered another vodka and another. When the veteran invited her to have a drink with him at his apartment, she declined. She then asked him if he would like to see her new apartment, and he declined. My guess is that, knowing she was becoming intoxicated, she wanted someone to accompany her in the cold and darkness to her new home lest she fall or lose her way. At about 7:00 P.M., she telephoned her friend Kate, whose apartment Terry had been sharing during the brief intervals when she was not in detox. Detecting that Terry had been drinking, Kate tried to find out where she was so that she could come and bring her home. Kate had earlier assured Terry that she would serve as her sponsor in the Alcoholics Anonymous recovery program, and would also be her landlord until she was ready for an apartment of her own.

But Terry declined to say where she was, perhaps not wanting her sponsor and friend to see her intoxicated and also preferring to go to her own new apartment. She then left the Crystal Corner Bar, either of her own volition or at the request of the bartender, and walked up Williamson Street, perhaps to buy the items she needed at the Sunshine Market at the other end of the block. In any event, she stopped en route at Jamaica Jo Mama's Restaurant and Bar, where she ordered another drink. Shortly before 8:00 P.M., she left Jamaica Jo's, absentmindedly failing to pay her check, which was then taken care of by a patron who had been sitting next to her. Turning into an open area adjoining the bar, she apparently fell into a snowbank. After getting up, covered with snow, she entered without knocking the back door of the house next to the bar.

Frederika Armson, a young single mother, was working in her kitchen when Terry quietly walked into her living room, where her two little children were chatting on the sofa. Jennifer Sandecke, another young woman who shared the small house, was also in the living room watching television. Frederika had been expecting her mother and assumed that the person who had walked into her house unannounced was she. After a brief pause, she went into the living room and found Jennifer and the children looking puzzled and trying to engage the unknown intruder in conversation.

Terry seemed unable to speak but stood quietly smiling at the children, who were about the same ages as her own daughters. Frederika and Jennifer asked Terry if she had been injured in an accident or if she was on medication, but she remained silent, continuing to smile affectionately at the children. Based on her previous history, it appears Terry was in an alcoholic blackout.

Frederika, who later described the stranger as "well groomed, gentle, and unthreatening," nonetheless ordered her children to go upstairs while she went to the phone to call 911. But as she conferred with the police, Terry quietly slipped out of the house through the front door onto Williamson Street. Jennifer later noted that Terry seemed to know how to move quickly, unlock the door, and leave easily, "as though she were familiar with the house." Frederika followed Terry out past the next-door Lakeside Press building and then down a narrow driveway toward the rear of that building; there Terry veered off to the left behind the house on that side of the driveway. Frederika pointed out this route to the police team that arrived a few minutes later, but they were unable to find her.

About half an hour after leaving the Armson house, around 8:30 P.M., Terry was encountered by a neighbor, Doneva Cox. Ms. Cox was headed for the nearby Sunshine Market when she noticed Terry, apparently inebriated, standing at the Lakeside Press driveway entrance. She asked her if she was drunk, to which Terry replied, "Yes."

"Do you know where you live?" inquired Ms. Cox. Terry answered, "No."

While the concerned woman watched, Terry walked slowly the fifty or so yards to the Crystal Corner Bar, where she had started the evening three hours earlier. She paused outside and then entered.

When I first talked to the manager by telephone several days later, he denied that anyone had seen Terry in his bar the night of her death. But when I arrived at the Crystal Corner unexpectedly a month later, two different bartenders talked rather nervously about her presence that night. Chris had served her after 5:00 P.M. until he went off duty at 7:00 P.M.; Todd, who began work at 7:00 P.M., said that Terry, after leaving the bar about then, returned obviously intoxicated at about 8:30 P.M. He said that he refused three times to serve her, prompting her to leave about five minutes after she arrived. No one claims to have seen her after she left the Crystal Corner Bar shortly after 8:30 P.M.

Police Officer Sue Armagost and a Detective Gebler arrived at the Armson residence around 8:00 P.M. and were told that Terry had left the house walking west. They began searching that area on foot, which should have included the space behind the Lakeside Press next door to the Armson house. They also inquired about Terry at the Crystal Bar, but were given no information there. Meanwhile, Police Officer Chris Smith arrived at the Armson house and interviewed Frederika and Jennifer in more detail about the behavior of the woman who had entered their house. They told Officer Smith that Terry "had snow all over her as if she had fallen, but she did not appear to be injured."

Officers Smith and Armagost then drove around the neighborhood before returning to the Armson home, at which point Smith searched on foot the area behind the buildings to the east of the house. It was during this search that the bartender at Jamaica Jo's told Smith of a woman fitting Terry's description who had left his bar earlier. Smith and Armagost also checked other bars, including Jolly Bob's, which was closed, and the Wisconsin Inn, where no one had seen a person fitting Terry's description. Why the police failed to find her in this little neighborhood where she had been a familiar figure for so many years remains a troubling mystery to me.

At 12:45 in the afternoon the next day, Tuesday, December 13, an employee at the Lakeside Press, Jerrold Chernow, opened the back door of the shop to check whether there was space available for his car in the small parking area.

"Hey," he said, "there's a little kid passed out in the snow." The owner of the shop, Norman Stockwell, a slender bearded man (who as a teenager had distributed my campaign literature in the Wisconsin presidential primary of 1972, as had Chernow), went out to check on the fallen child.

"It's not a kid," Stockwell called out. "And whoever it is seems to be a lot more than just passed out. There's no pulse. Call 911," he shouted. Chernow phoned, but apparently did not hear all of Stockwell's observations; he told the 911 operator that he had found a child of approximately thirteen years of age without a pulse. *Washington Post* writer Laura Blumenfeld described the scene:

The fingers were frozen hard. Her skin was colorless. Her socks had iced onto her feet. She lay next to a circle of footprints, a ring ten feet in diameter, her own sneakered prints tamped down upon each other, as if she had been trying to walk straight but could only make dizzy circles until she dropped.

It was just after noon on December 13, raw and overcast in Madison, Wisconsin. In the minutes it took for the emergency crew to arrive, the printer . . . knelt and covered the body with his coat.

There's something about this woman, he thought. She had a delicate, poetic face. There was refinement to her, the dangling earrings, the russet hair smoothed into a barrette.

She had no purse, no ID; she had fallen among garbage cans and dead sunflowers. Still, he was certain; this woman had a home.

Her gloves were missing, probably left in one of the bars. Her scarf had fallen to the ground in a car track eight or ten feet from her body. There was nothing in her pockets other than the key to her apartment and five $1 bills. She wore a wristwatch, two rings—one silver and one gold—and her beloved earrings. The 911 emergency crew, the police, and Deputy Coroner Philip Little, who examined Terry where she lay in the snow, quickly determined that she was dead. They had her body transported to St. Mary's Hospital, where she had been treated only six days earlier, and where an autopsy would be performed the next day at 2:00 P.M. They then reported to the news media that an unidentified woman had been found. Later that afternoon, two staff members at the detox center Terry had just checked out of the day before heard the report on the radio. Melody Music-Twilla and Gerry Kluever, counselors who had worked with Terry during her confinements at the center in recent years, suspected the unknown dead woman might be Terry. Melody telephoned the coroner's office about 5:30 P.M., and Little, the deputy coroner, who had photographed Terry's body at St. Mary's, suggested that he bring the pictures to the detox center for identification.

Half an hour later, Melody and Gerry gazed at the Polaroid and began to weep. There was Terry "looking as though she were simply sleeping"—the same vulnerable, delicate person who had left the center in high hopes only a few hours before.

ALL INDICATIONS ARE that after leaving the Crystal Corner Bar, Terry trudged the half block back to the print shop and walked into the driveway to the parking space just a few paces from the house she had entered thirty-five or forty minutes earlier. After wandering in a circle, she either lay down or fell into the snow, where bitter cold began asserting its claim. Doctors tell me that after initial chills and shivering she would soon begin to feel warm. Her body heat melted the seven inches of snow all the way down to the grass. But as the biting cold slowed her bodily functions, her heartbeat began to grow faint, and then it stopped. There was simply too much snow and cold fighting against too small a body, despite its tenacious and plucky heart.

Given the intense cold that night, Terry may have died before midnight of December 12, but since her body was not discovered until shortly after noon the next day, her death was officially recorded as of December 13. "Death due to hypothermia while in a state of extreme intoxication," according to the coroner's report.

I DO NOT expect ever to read sadder words of finality. They force me to face so many questions about Terry's life and death. What could I have done differently? What if I had been a more concerned and actively involved parent when she was a little girl, or a fragile adolescent? Why wasn't I in closer touch with her in the final months? Knowing that alcoholism is a dangerous, often fatal disease, should I have intervened to have her committed indefinitely to a locked-door long-term-treatment facility?

More immediate questions also persist. Why couldn't the police find an intoxicated young woman wandering only a few steps from where the 911 call was made? Why did the bartenders and patrons at two bars let her go out alone into the subfreezing darkness obviously intoxicated?

Perhaps in the festive atmosphere of the Christmas season, people were thinking about their own pleasures and family concerns rather than the well-being of a stranger who was drinking too much. Perhaps others were a little high themselves from too many toasts to a merry Christmas. Perhaps there is an understandable tendency for people to avoid becoming involved with intoxicated people, who can behave unpredictably and offensively. Perhaps it is unrealistic to expect people to carry even momentarily the burdens of some other person's drinking problem.

Of one fact I am certain: if Terry's role had been reversed with some of the people who encountered her that night, she would have done her best to guide the person in trouble on a path to safety. Frederika Armson did her best in calling 911, and she later told me that although Terry could not speak that evening in her living room, Terry left her with a sense of having been "blessed" by her quiet and gently smiling presence.

When I expressed my concerns about these matters to an old family friend well acquainted with Terry's unfailing compassion and sensitive nature, he responded: "George, in this tragedy, as in so much of our lives, the luck factor is often decisive."

Terry had been lucky many times in her life—other people had often come to her rescue when she was in trouble. Her luck ran out in the cold of that Christmastide evening.

The luck factor is underscored by two actions on the part of the two men at the print shop, Stockwell and Chernow. Stockwell had left work at 6:30 P.M. on December 12 but returned around 8:45 P.M., parking his car on the street in front of his shop. If he had used the parking area at the rear of his shop, it is quite possible that he would have encountered Terry either wandering in that space or lying in the snow spotlighted by his headlights. If she had arrived later with his car parked in that area, he would doubtless have discovered her when he left work a second time late that evening.

Chernow, who had left work at 7:15 P.M. from the rear parking area, is certain that Terry was not there at that time, or he would have caught her in the beam of his headlights. In the park-

ing area, in addition to his car, were an old disabled car belonging to Stockwell and a van belonging to someone at the University of Wisconsin. It was difficult for Chernow to maneuver
in the snow past the van, so the next morning he parked his car
on the street in front of the shop. It is unlikely that Terry was
still alive that morning when Chernow arrived at work, but we
cannot be sure. It was four hours later when he discovered her
body while checking to see if the van had left, making room for
him to move his car in from the street.

And there was a third piece of bad luck. A light on the rear
of the building had been broken by mischievous youngsters a
couple of nights earlier, leaving the parking area in darkness.
Had the light been working, it would have illuminated the area
the night of Terry's entrance, making it more likely that
the searching police would find her, and if she was attempting to hide, she might not have considered this a safe hiding
place.

Of course, absent a successful intervention and recovery,
Terry was living on borrowed time. The central question about
her life and death does not turn on a failure of luck in the last
hours of her life. The question is, how did a beautiful, endearing, quick-witted, compassionate, and perceptive little girl grow
up to become an alcoholic powerless to control or save her life?
Why wasn't she one of the fortunate ones who through medical
diagnosis and the AA program are able to recover from the disease?

These questions have haunted me since that late-night ringing of my doorbell. If I have found even partial answers, it is
because I have pursued Terry's story with a loving heart and a
questioning mind over the forty-five years of her life. I must
confess that while I loved and cherished this special daughter
since she was a small child, it took her death, the amazingly con-
sistent testimony of her friends, and her candid letters and jour-

nals to open my eyes fully to the fact that Teresa Jane Mc-
Govern was all along one of the most lovable and loving human
beings on this troubled earth. I do not believe that she needed
to die. I regret terribly that she did. But perhaps in God's good
time I shall come to see a redeeming purpose to this death in
the snow.

The McGovern family (from left to right: Mary, Steve, me, Eleanor, Ann, Susan, and Terry) at our Coquelin Terrace home in Chevy Chase, Maryland, in 1959.

T W O

"My three favorite people are God,
Jesus, and Adlai Stevenson."

"HEY, HARPIE, YOU son of a bitch. Hey, Harpie, you god-damn witch." And then excited giggles in the background from childish throats hidden from view.

I couldn't believe what I was hearing. My four-year-old daughter peering out an open window and hurling such shocking—albeit dramatically poetic—profanity against our next-door neighbor, the elderly and proper Mrs. Harper.

Shirtless and perspiring in the Dakota July heat, I abandoned the lawn mower and raced into the house—partly to silence the offending voice and partly to escape the withering glare of Mrs. Harper. I had sensed earlier that she was slightly offended by my sweating half-naked body, even before she came under direct assault from my fearless child.

Immediately, I found the source of the explosive language. Eight-year-old Ann and seven-year-old Sue were lying low on the floor coaching their little sister Terry in the next vile epithet to be tossed out the window.

How could I, a college history professor in his first job at a Methodist college, Dakota Wesleyan, ever live this down? Would anyone believe that such language was not countenanced in the McGovern household—especially when aimed at so impeccable a target as Mrs. Harper?

Clearly, this was a case for parental discipline. But if you knew Mrs. Harper, you might forgive me for confessing that, even yet, this scene of forty years ago makes me chuckle as I contemplate the wicked ingenuity of Ann and Susan and the unquestioning bravery of Terry, their junior mouthpiece.

Of course, I wondered where my young daughters had picked up this profanity and the nerve to use it. Certainly not from their gentle mother, Eleanor, nor from me—a World War II pilot who had been steeped a few years earlier in the highly specialized, nonstop, four-letter-word language of military life, but never used it around my family or other civilians without extensive combat experience. I suspected Bob McCardle, the rough-talking, flamboyant basketball coach at Dakota Wesleyan—a frequent bachelor dinner guest at our house whose florid accounts of what he had told his players at halftime or offending referees in close games sometimes penetrated the playroom or bedrooms of our children.

Coach McCardle, a big, bluff, broad-shouldered, somewhat menacing man who loved to talk, also loved our kids—especially Terry, who could always be counted on to perform attention-getting rituals for him with a little goading on his part. With this willing four-year-old player at center stage in the middle of our living room, and her older sisters looking on enviously, the coach would take her through her paces, all the time rocking with laughter. He had her primed and eager to cooperate in the more imaginative and bolder coaching ventures by her sisters. Whether or not Mrs. Harper ever forgave us for the resulting outrage is not known, but we later heard that she had observed, "What can you expect from those Democrats!"

Our only son, Steven, had made his arrival in 1952, three years behind Terry; Mary followed Steve by three years in 1955 to complete our family of four girls and one boy. The years in Mitchell, South Dakota, were happy ones for our children, as were the graduate-school years that dovetailed with them in Evanston, Illinois. Following World War II and thirty-five bombing missions over Nazi Germany as a B-24 pilot, I had joined Eleanor in Mitchell, where I had grown up as a boy and where Eleanor and I had met while we were both freshmen at Dakota Wesleyan in 1941. The Japanese had bombed Pearl Harbor on December 7 of that year, and I quickly volunteered for service as a pilot with the Army Air Corps. We were married on Halloween Day, October 31, 1943, in the small Methodist church of Eleanor's hometown, Woonsocket, South Dakota, after I had managed a three-day pass from pilot training at Muskogee, Oklahoma. Eleanor was with me through successive training stages at Coffeeville, Kansas; Pampa, Texas; Liberal, Kansas; Lincoln, Nebraska; and Mountain Home, Idaho.

It was at Mountain Home that a stubborn round-the-clock nausea attacked Eleanor. An Air Corps doctor diagnosed her illness as diabetes and prescribed daily insulin shots and a severely restricted diet. After she experienced insulin shock, the doctor called me to the hospital, gave me authorization for an emergency pass as well as instructions in insulin injection, and ordered me to take Eleanor back to South Dakota on the next train. Dr. J. H. Lloyd, our hometown doctor, after reading a detailed letter from the hapless Air Corps physician, turned to me in disgust and declared: "This man is an idiot. Tell Eleanor to throw away that insulin and start eating anything she wants. Bring her in so that I can examine her. . . . She is going to have a baby— not diabetes." Dr. Lloyd delivered Ann on March 10, 1945, at the Methodist State Hospital in Mitchell, where all five of our children were to be born.

It was also at this same hospital that Eleanor's beautiful mother, Marian, had died following surgery just ten years earlier. Marian was thirty-four at the time; Eleanor and her twin sister, Ila, were eleven years old. The death was not handled well by her devastated father and other family adults. They seemed oblivious to the fact that eleven-year-olds also grieve and need extra reassurance and emotional support when they have suddenly lost their mother. Eleanor was devoted to her father, but he remained so saddened by his wife's death that he had little inclination to consider the needs of his motherless children. Eleanor suffered the consequences at no time more painfully than during her pregnancy and the period following Terry's birth on June 10, 1949.

Terry was an unusually beautiful and engaging baby, weighing six pounds and fourteen ounces—"a perfect little porcelain doll," exclaimed an admiring artist friend of ours. But her young mother went into a postpartum depression that afflicted her for long painful months after Terry's birth. All of us have days when we are "down" or "blue," but these experiences are not serious. Clinical depression is beyond the comprehension of those who have not experienced it. Later, Eleanor sought professional help for this recurring affliction. Always, the psychiatrists pointed to the unresolved conflicts and fears stemming from her mother's death.

The birth of Teresa, Eleanor's third daughter, may have revived memories that her mother had died of complications following the birth of her third daughter. Eleanor was haunted as a child by her father's description of a vivid dream he had in which he saw her with her deceased mother in the afterlife. Listening to this story unfold, Eleanor heard her grandmother say: "Oh dear, I hope that does not mean that Eleanor is going to die too." For years Eleanor feared that this was actually what the dream had foretold.

I had one more year of graduate school at Northwestern, but we had come home to Mitchell for the summer of '49 so that I could gain a summer term of teaching history at Dakota Wesleyan. I was absorbed in my doctoral dissertation, but not too absorbed to worry about Eleanor, who was struggling to maintain her health while caring for a new baby and two energetic little girls, Ann and Susan, ages four and three.

We were not capable then—nor are we now—of evaluating the impact of Eleanor's depression on our children, but she had an underlying emotional strength, high intelligence, and incredible patience. During the decade from 1945 to 55, when she was giving birth to and carefully nurturing five babies, she did what was expected of women in this era: she prepared their meals with a constant eye on sound nutrition, made their dresses and coats, looked after their medical and dental needs, laundered and ironed their clothes, read stories to them, looked after their school needs, took them on adventurous recreational excursions, and kept the house in good order. I helped from time to time with these matters, but Eleanor carried the major load, with no hired assistance except on special occasions. For enjoyment, she liked nothing better than to work in her beloved flower garden to the point of exhaustion. She also diligently digested daily newspapers and devoured magazines and books—all of which left her the best-informed woman in town, if sometimes the weariest. If you wanted to make Eleanor furious in those days, all you had to do was observe that she was lucky not to have to work— meaning a job outside the home. To Eleanor, no job but home-making and rearing a family required so high a level of wisdom, imagination, humor, character, and strength.

Years later, Terry developed the same convictions. It seemed to me that she came to envy her mother's life—sometimes to the point of resentment and anger. She told me several times that she would gladly have opted as Eleanor did for getting married at twenty-one to a husband who loved her and provided a secure income. She would also have welcomed five babies by the

time she was thirty-one, a comfortable house, and no professional career worries. She tasted none of these fulfilling experiences until the last nine years of her life—and then only in part,
under difficult and sometimes painful circumstances. Despite
occasional outbursts against her mother, Terry loved her dearly
and spent countless hours with her discussing her concerns and
aspirations. Keenly aware of Eleanor's sense of loss stemming
from the untimely death of her mother, Terry named her first
daughter, Marian, after her.

Eleanor's strength came through during the summer of 1952,
when I was a full professor at Dakota Wesleyan. With three-
year-old Terry and her two older sisters under foot as well as a
baby on the way, Eleanor typed and retyped my 450-page doctoral dissertation without a single uncorrected typographical
error. She was working on the final pages when labor pains
began announcing the imminent arrival of Steve on July 27,
1952. This enforced typing until the last hours of pregnancy was
doubtless close to if not over the line into spousal abuse!

With Steve born, my dissertation—"The Colorado Coal
Strike, 1913–1914"—out of the way, the Ph.D. in history
awarded at Northwestern, and Eleanor and our children happily
looking on, life was usually good for the young McGovern family, both in Evanston and Mitchell, except for Eleanor's recurring bouts with depression. There were numerous late afternoons
or weekends for visits to parks, playgrounds, and zoos and the
Lake Michigan shoreline of Evanston and adjoining Chicago. In
Mitchell, we had easy access to Hitchcock Park, a lovely place
for picnics, swimming, swings, teeter-totters, slides, and sand-
boxes. There were frequent visits to the beach at Lake Mitchell;
while a small child, Terry took lessons and became a superb
swimmer with a well-coordinated stroke. She loved the water
and swimming for the rest of her life.

Many years later, writing in her journal in 1990, a period of recovery marked by nearly a year of sobriety, Terry wrote a tale based on her idealized picture of what she wished her childhood had been like:

Once upon a time, there was a little girl born to an already fulfilled mother and father. Her birth brought them even more fulfillment as they were eager to give of what they had received as children and adults. She was a delightful child and could feel herself grow on her insides every time she learned something new or could make someone laugh, and she could see that those in her family were happy for her growth.

Sometimes at night she had scary dreams and woke up hot all over. It would feel all right as soon as she remembered where she was—though sometimes she had to crawl in bed between her mom and dad—or, if she wanted to cuddle in the safety of just one of them, she could. Always, one of them would murmur, "Are you all right, Terry?" She knew if she just needed to be touched in a special way, sung to, softly spoken to; if she wanted to talk or if she wanted to be quiet, she could have it.

Sometimes she felt so safe and loved that as soon as the scary, electric feelings left her body, she'd walk back to her room and nestle like a puppy in the warmth of her quilt, feather pillow, and big stuffed bear. The rain came down one night and she could hear its steady rhythm. It began almost as she slid under the blankets and closed her eyes. What it felt like was an angel kissing her on her forehead and then resting on her nightstand to be with her through the night.

Starting school was a strange thing. As much as her mom and dad and sisters spent time with her helping her to imagine what it was like, there was a tight and scared spot in her tummy. Every time that tightness came, she'd go to someone in her family and tell them about it. The tight feeling that was really loneliness and fear would go away. She always felt she could find someone in her family to go to about anything.

There were times, of course, when everyone seemed busy, but when that happened, she was told something she could do to help her tightness and reassured she was not alone and they could be with her soon. When that happened, sometimes it worked so well, starting to do whatever was suggested, that she forgot she needed to be with someone. She didn't have words for it until she was older, but what she was doing was trusting in their love and strength, taking that into her aloneness, and finding herself in herself.

Sometimes someone would say, "I can't talk or spend time with you now, but I can in a half hour. Would it help to go pick some flowers in the garden?—try to see if there is anything else in nature that looks like that flower."

Once I picked a pansy and told my father it looked like a little girl's face with a bonnet tied under her chin. He broke out into a big grin, hugged me, and said, "That was very fine, seeing what a creative girl I am blessed with."

One of the things she liked best was that her father really loved her mother. She could tell that because he was home a lot. There weren't many dinners where he was gone. He wanted to know about her day, about all of his children's days. And he listened, laughed, or showed sadness if it was a sad day for someone. All of us would try and listen to each other. Mama told us it was OK if we couldn't—whether it was because someone was too tired, too excited, or whatever, we'd just say so. What was not OK was to make fun of, hurt, or take attention from another when they were talking. So the little girl didn't really feel very scared at all when she was talking about her day. She loved that.

She liked that her mom and dad got their turn to tell how their days were. Not only did they get a turn, but it really seemed to the little girl that they wanted her to know them too. Their touch, their laughter, their anger, their sadness, their listening was something familiar and safe.

There was a little girl in her class, her best friend, whose family was not like this. Her name was Grace. The little girl thought that Grace was so pretty, so witty and creative, and did not understand why Grace's sisters did not like this about her. Instead, they left her feeling ashamed, scared, and lonely by the things they said to her. One time when Grace was being very funny and warm with the adults in her home—her parents and aunt and uncle—one of Grace's sisters said, "You think you're so cute, but you're not," in her meanest voice. Grace put her head down and walked to her room. The little girl hurt for her friend. She would go to her when things like this happened or when Grace felt lonely. She would try to give her some of the things she had received from her own family. She could see that it helped, and she loved her friend all the more for letting her give her a gift—her attention.

At least during the Mitchell years before we moved to Washington, this warm recollection of Terry's childish years is not far removed from my recollection of the reality of her childhood. But, sadly, this is not the view Terry carried in her mind. The final paragraph about the little girl's friend Grace is actually how Terry saw herself as a child—her recollections of the resentment she sometimes felt. In her journal entry of November 9, 1992, Terry relates that she had just read this little story to seven-year-old Marian:

I read my "once upon a time there was a little girl" story to Marian. I wonder if it was all right, especially to tell her that my sisters were so jealous of me. . . . Marian might have been afraid when I said, "Part of why my sisters were jealous is that I was my dad's favorite," because she knows she is my dad's favorite of the grandchildren.

I've tried to avoid favoritism with my children and grandchildren. I also believe that Terry exaggerated her siblings' resentment. But she normally spoke her mind candidly; her story represents her honest perceptions.

Eleanor and I were, of course, heavily involved in other concerns in those years. We shared a keen interest in politics—especially the 1952 presidential campaign. The intelligent, witty, and principled Democratic nominee, Adlai Stevenson, became our hero; indeed, our new son, Steven, was named after him. Stevenson said during that campaign, "Better to lose the election than to mislead the people." And again, "There are some things worse than losing an election." We were to draw consolation from those lines twenty years later.

Some measure of the conversation about Stevenson around our house was an exchange Eleanor and I overheard between four-year-old Terry and a neighborhood playmate who proclaimed that his favorite people were his mother, his dad, and his baby sister. "They're not my favorite people," Terry retorted. "My favorites are God, Jesus, and Adlai Stevenson." When I later had occasion to relate this story to Stevenson, he responded: "That's a wonderful story, George, but I don't believe that you and I together could sell that version of the Holy Trinity!"

In June 1953, still inspired by the Stevenson campaign, I accepted an invitation from the South Dakota Democratic state chairman, Ward Clark, to become the full-time executive secretary of the South Dakota Democratic Party. Resigning as professor of history, I continued for two and a half more years to coach the college's debate squad while devoting my major energies to building a Democratic Party in largely one-party Republican South Dakota.

This combination of duties involved constant travel that took me away from the family much of the time. It was an early introduction to the conflict between politics and normal family life. I was not sufficiently aware of this problem at the time.

I have noted, however, that many fathers of my generation in business, law, medicine, or journalism, or in physical labor, spent no more time guiding their children, playing with them, working with them, or just enjoying them than I did. Leaving the care of the children to the mother while Dad brought home the paycheck was the norm then. That system was not all bad; at least it gave children the advantage of one parent at home. My children also tell me that they were proud of the work I was doing and appreciated my good humor when I was home. I think

Eleanor and I provided models to our children of social conscience, decency and tolerance in human relations, a love for books and music and cultural affairs, and a constant concern for their well-being.

Looking back, I can now recognize some flaws in our parenting and in our spousal relations, but such faults have probably existed in most families since the Garden of Eden. By and large, I believe, the McGovern household was a pretty good place to be. Terry's death has powerfully brought home to us not only how much we loved her but also how much we love and treasure one another.

When my party-building efforts got under way that hot summer of 1953, the South Dakota legislature was composed of 2 Democrats and 108 Republicans. Thus, we had a two-party system of sorts, but the ratio of Democrats to Republicans was what most of my fellow South Dakotans thought appropriate. Two and a half years later, we had a much more vigorous and well-organized party with a more appealing message, and I was elected to the U.S. Congress—the first Democrat to win high office in South Dakota in a quarter of a century.

It was an uphill battle with an unbelievably small budget and no paid staff. Winning that race against an entrenched incumbent Congressman, Harold Lovre—one of the strongest vote-getters in the South Dakota Republican Party—is still one of my proudest achievements. Every one of my children except one-year-old Mary—later to become a star McGovern campaigner and strategist—participated in the campaign, as, of course, did Eleanor, always my most effective public advocate. We ran that entire race on a budget of $12,000, ending with a debt of $5,000 that Eleanor and I paid off ourselves during my first two years in Congress, when congressional salaries were $22,000 annually.

Terry carved out her own role, which consisted of hand-delivering my posters to local merchants for display. Whenever she discovered a poster of my opponent already displayed ahead of her visit, she would try to persuade the merchant to replace it with mine, contending that she and her friends would guarantee more business for stores carrying the magical McGovern label.

As the campaign progressed and Terry overheard worried conversations between her parents about campaign finances, she opened her piggy bank and purchased candy bars to sell from a neighborhood makeshift stand she assembled herself. She pledged the proceeds to the McGovern for Congress Campaign Committee. Her business acumen did not quite equal her campaign enthusiasm, however—she purchased the candy bars for ten cents apiece and sold them for the same price. If a potential buyer could not afford full price, she quickly arranged a discount. With Terry, throughout her life, compassion was always more important than money or personal profit. But let me tell you, though I was the recipient of tens of millions of dollars in campaign contributions over the next quarter of a century, no one ever gave me a contribution that I treasured or used more carefully than those dimes from my little seven-year-old daughter in that first race so many years ago.

I have literally tons of political memorabilia that have accumulated over time, including photos of me with the leading political and international figures of our age. But one photo I value especially is of a tiny homemade float: Ann, Susan, Terry, and Steve riding in two child's wagons towed by a miniature tractor driven by an older neighborhood boy of twelve. They are riding in a parade in Mitchell proudly holding a hand-lettered banner: MCGOVERN FOR CONGRESS, 1956. If you think that display of love and courage from one's children does not matter to a candidate—especially in an uphill race with little money—you do not grasp the power of emotional support in determining the outcome of an election. I have been blessed over the years by South Dakota supporters and backers across the nation who gave me their hearts as well as their votes. It has made the difference repeatedly in elections. But no backer, however powerful, has meant more to me than my own children and Eleanor.

I always disliked the more flamboyant aspects of politics, such as displaying myself on the back of a convertible or pickup truck riding in a parade and waving and grinning endlessly to the citizenry along the way. My wife and children despised such theatrics too, but they went along with them anyway, knowing that they are part of life in a political family. If I had my career to live over again I would minimize these antics, especially for my family.

I know of the unsettling and demoralizing impact on children of having their father assailed or ridiculed by political critics. There is no escape from this aspect of American politics. In my first congressional race I was assailed in full-page newspaper ads for betraying the nation to communism because I had advocated American diplomatic recognition of China—the same step we had taken as far back as 1933 with Russia. Such attacks never ceased. In my final race for the U.S. Senate, political opponents called me a baby-killer because I refused to support an amendment to the Constitution making abortion a federal crime. The father of five children and the husband of the same wife for thirty-seven years, I was given a zero rating by a group advertising itself as pro-family. My victorious opponent, a fifty-eight-year-old bachelor, was given a 100 percent rating for his advancement of family values!

My children handled such matters in their own way, with what reassurance we could provide. I think they adopted a protective stance toward their parents—a fierce loyalty to family— against the often threatening world that surrounded us. In a democracy, it is the public and those forces that influence the public that hold the reins in determining the political family's course. I never thanked my son and daughters enough for their grace and effort in all of this. I pray that they will read these words with some sense of the increasing admiration and appreciation I feel toward them dating back to campaigns together since 1956.

AT CHRISTMASTIME, FOLLOWING my 1956 election, Eleanor and I loaded our five children into a new Ford station wagon and headed for Washington, D.C. With the help of my friend Hubert Humphrey, a South Dakota native, who had just completed his first term as a senator from his adopted Minnesota, we purchased a home next door to the Humphreys at 3214 Coquelin Terrace in Chevy Chase, Maryland, where we were to live for the next twelve years.

Terry, seven years old when we moved to our new home, quickly developed a special affinity for our neighbor, whom she dubbed "Humfey." You could watch the two of them bantering frequently in our adjoining front yards and driveways. Hubert was one of the most active and heavily involved senators on the national stage, but he always seemed to find a few minutes for the kids of our neighborhood, and Terry was clearly one of his favorites. The feeling was mutual. If a politician was humane and humorous, he was two-thirds of the way into Terry's heart for good. Hubert was both of these and so much more, and Terry dearly loved him and his wife, Muriel, as well as the Humphrey children—especially the youngest member, Douglas, her soul mate in the Humphrey family.

Years later, after the Vietnam War had placed Hubert and me on opposing sides in the competition for the 1972 Democratic presidential nomination, Terry's love for Hubert continued despite her fierce loyalty to her father. For Terry, and all our children, it was more fun campaigning against Richard Nixon in the fall—even though it was a losing effort—than participating in the spring victories over Hubert, Ed Muskie, Scoop Jackson, Terry Sanford, John Lindsay, Shirley Chisholm, and the other Democratic contenders. In a journal entry of May 26, 1984, several years after Hubert had died of cancer, Terry described a dream she had of a political parade in Mitchell, South Dakota:

> *HHH was there and I really wanted to get to him. Knew he'd be glad to see me. He always liked me and made me feel very special—called me the Queen of Coquelin Terrace.*

Terry and me in our Washington home, 1968.

THREE

"He called me the Queen of Coquelin Terrace."

THE COMFORTABLE FOUR-BEDROOM brick houses that lined each side of the arching street were for the most part occupied by young parents with four, five, or six children—typical of post–World War II American families. Indeed, so many children scurried around Coquelin Terrace that it was dubbed the Fertile Crescent. Coquelin Terrace is a little horseshoe street with the two ends opening onto Jones Mill Road just a couple of blocks north of the East-West Highway, a much-traveled Washington-area artery. It is adjacent to Washington's Rock Creek Park, with its lovely tree-lined stream that babbles and flows over a rocky base through much of the Washington area, helping to make the nation's capital one of the world's most beautiful cities. When we lived on Coquelin, it offered pleasant middle-class homes constructed by an eccentric Belgian lancer turned contractor who lived at midpoint on the horseshoe, Joe Geeraert.

The house was never quite large enough for our family, so Eleanor and I constantly enlarged it, first by converting the attic to a bright, attractive dormer bedroom for Ann and Susan, to which they gained entry by a pull-down stairway opening to our second-floor hallway. That access system was a little awkward, but it was the envy of the neighborhood kids. We then converted the carport to a cozy den where I could read and write and keep my constantly expanding library and files. Largely for Eleanor's pleasure, we glassed in our back screened porch and upgraded it into a pleasant sitting and reading room where we could relax and view Eleanor's gorgeous garden. We had previously constructed a large stone patio that she—always the gardener and South Dakota farm girl—covered with roses, tulips, pansies, daisies, zinnias, and other flowers and shrubbery, plus her ever lovingly tended bird feeders.

For Mary, a year and a half old when we moved to Washington, we constructed a built-in bed in an alcove of the smallest bedroom. It was an ideal room for a little girl, but in a few years it began to press in on its growing, lively, fun-loving occupant, although she never complained. Mary was the darling of the family. Everybody's heart was at her disposal.

Steve—"Burr Head," as I called him because of his close-cropped hair—had a somewhat larger bedroom, where he built up a huge collection of toy soldiers that he played with endlessly, placing them in elaborate battle formations as he carefully re-fought the battles of the Civil War. He needed no playtime with his sisters to keep happily occupied. In family discussions recalling those earlier years, Steve has always contended that his childhood days were completely happy. He experienced no sense of neglect from anyone, including his frequently absent dad.

Across the hall was Terry's bedroom, which she cherished and constantly cleaned and rearranged. It was not uncommon for her, at any time of the day or night, to empty all the drawers, neatly place everything back in order, move the furniture into different arrangements, clean the closet from top to bottom, vacuum every inch of the rug thoroughly, rearrange her pictures on the walls and dresser, and lovingly check each one of her earrings, bracelets, necklaces, and trinkets to make sure it was in the exact order she preferred in her jewelry box. She was a compulsive cleaner and arranger. And she loved that room above all other possessions. That was "Ter the Bear's" lair.

Many years later in her journal entry of October 14, 1987, she reflected on her growing-up years: "If parents provide safety, I know I had times of it—being in my dad's presence—being with Mom while she dressed for the evening. My room became my haven—the only place I could control. Without that, I was lost. . . ."

In the spring of 1994 when I asked her if she had found a job to enable her to pay the rent on her apartment in Wisconsin, she said, "No, Dad, but I'm cleaning up my apartment every day, which makes me feel like I'm worth at least something." I've always suspected that the frequent unmanageability of Terry's life prompted a countertactic: if I can't organize my life, I can at least organize my room or living space.

Recognizing her special affection for her childhood room, Eleanor and I splurged a little and bought her a matching set of bedroom furniture—bed, dressing table, bookshelves, desk, and large bureau with ample drawer space. It came in a soft beige with light green trim, but at Terry's suggestion we later painted it a soft blue. She cherished that furniture and kept it in use or safe in storage for the rest of her life. It has now been passed on to her daughters.

Nearby, "Candy Cane City"—a wonderful children's play area and picnic ground at our end of Rock Creek Park—was a magical place for Terry. It had a great assortment of children's play equipment, rides, and a nearby stable where you could engage a riding horse or pony. Our family spent hundreds of happy hours there, and no one enjoyed those times more than Terry.

She also loved to visit Dr. Packett's drugstore, which included Ponder's soda and lunch counter, located in a small shopping center within an easy walk of our house. This was where she spent most of her monthly allowance. I can still see her considering what to buy from Dr. Packett's eclectic shop, or from Ponder's magical lunch counter. One day, Eleanor noticed that Terry had come home with items clearly beyond the reach of her allowance. After hard questioning, she admitted that she had experimented with shoplifting. With Terry in tow, we marched her back to the store and witnessed her apology and return of the merchandise to Dr. Packett. It was a painful and humiliating experience for Terry, one that she mentioned to me thirty years later as though it had happened last week.

Near the end of her life when she would run out of money and her craving for alcohol was beyond control, she occasionally took beer or vodka from a store without paying. Except for that, Terry was always honest and frugal. She handled her own money and any assistance we gave her in an economical manner. Her expenditures for clothing, personal effects, and household conveniences were always modest. When Eleanor would invite her to go shopping for a new dress or coat, Terry invariably rejected anything she regarded as expensive or extravagant. She worried about the medical care and treatment costs incurred by us as a result of her alcoholism.

DURING MY YEARS in the House and in the losing 1960 Senate race against longtime Republican Senator Karl Mundt, our family made several trips by car to South Dakota. In some cases Eleanor would drive all five of the children and our pets there in our station wagon while I remained for last-hour roll calls and then flew to the state to join them. It now amazes me to recall Eleanor's willing assumption of the heavy responsibility and stress of those fifteen-hundred-mile trips before any of the children were old enough to assist with the driving.

On one of the return auto trips when I was doing the driving, complete with the entire family plus a dog and two cats, we stopped overnight to visit my sister Mildred and her husband, Harold Brady, a Methodist minister, in Reedsburg, Wisconsin. In a letter to Terry's daughters dated May 8, 1995, my sister recalls an incident from this trip when Terry was twelve years old.

The morning they were to leave, their big fluffy gray cat squeezed himself into a hole behind the bathtub. There was barely room for him and no way for anyone to get him out until he decided to come. Each of us tried our luck at coaxing him out, but to no avail. Your Grampa George figured out how long it would take them to drive to the place where he was to deliver a speech that day and said if the cat didn't come out by a certain time they would have to leave him behind. We were to eat breakfast, and then it would be time for them to leave to meet the deadline.

Terry seemed particularly disturbed about the thought of leaving part of her family behind. I noticed that she didn't eat much breakfast and soon asked to be excused to go to the bathroom. After a little while a smiling Terry emerged carrying her big gray kitty. She had wrapped her bacon in her napkin and taken it with her to the bathroom. With the bacon she coaxed her cat out. He was content after his breakfast of bacon and she didn't let him out of her arms until her whole family and the pets were in the car with the doors closed. I'm sure the rest of the journey was happier for everyone because gray kitty was with them.

Terry quickly developed a number of friends in the Coquelin neighborhood—especially with a neighbor a couple of houses away, Morreen Bush. As they moved through the elementary years into Kensington Junior High, they became the closest of friends and confidantes. Morreen told me later that although she was a year older, "Terry was always the leader; I was the follower. She constantly had us laughing, always coming up with fun things to do. The interesting, imaginative, and happy memories of my childhood I owe almost entirely to Terry. If she was ever depressed or downhearted, I never saw it. All I can recall of my growing-up years with Terry is her marvelous wit, her creative ideas, her fascinating ways of expressing herself, and her kindness to everyone she met. I knew of no one who didn't like her, and by the time we finished junior high, half the boys in the neighborhood were in love with her."

Terry later shared with Morreen her concern that her older sisters might resent the manner in which she became the center of attention both at home and in the neighborhood. She was pleased that she had a special role in my life, but she also sometimes worried that her siblings might resent it. These concerns aside, she loved her friends and her role in their lives on Coquelin and at Kensington Junior High.

Before moving to Washington, Terry had completed her first year of schooling in Mitchell and was halfway through the second grade. Entering the North Chevy Chase Elementary School at the midpoint of the school year, she made the adjustment without apparent difficulty and did comparatively well throughout the elementary grades. Maryland's Montgomery County schools were then introducing the "new math," which caused some problems for transfer students such as Terry. She and her younger brother, Steve, had some trouble with this system. I was relieved to find a tutor who could make more sense of it than I was capable of doing.

In 1959, my mother came to Washington to spend a month with us. She had suffered a stroke in 1946 that left her unable to speak. Noting that a few involuntary words might be projected by her grandmother and responding warmly to her smiles and nods of approval, Terry, age ten, decided to teach her grandmother to speak again.

I had years earlier tried through Northwestern University's school of speech to determine if therapy might help my mother recover her speech. This effort failed to produce any improvement. But Terry was undaunted. Day after day she devoted time to her grandmother, showing her how to mouth certain words and sometimes putting her fingers to her patient's lips to demonstrate how certain words could be projected. These efforts failed to restore the power of speech. But they clearly brought an appreciative and affectionate response from my mother.

Shortly after her thirteenth birthday, Terry experienced some new thrills that were both joyful and hazardous: she acquired her first serious boyfriend and she discovered alcohol. His name was Bill, and he was to fill that role for several years—which turned out to be unfortunate for Terry.

The families around Coquelin Terrace included many World War II veterans, some of whom had become heavy drinkers during the war. Almost every house had a bar. Every weekend someone had a neighborhood cocktail party. It was taken for granted that after a hard week it was okay to have a few drinks—or as many as you wanted. Alcohol ensured a relaxed, sometimes boisterous evening for neighbors who went their separate ways during the week.

I don't recall anyone talking about "alcoholism." But I recall many laughing references to Bill or Mary or Bob "getting loaded," or "tying one on," or "getting smashed." And in later years we would learn that some of our old Coquelin friends had died too young from illnesses we now associate with alcoholism. The participation of Eleanor and me in such parties seemed restrained to some of our neighbors. Then as now, we would have been classified as moderate, occasional social drinkers—perhaps a vodka tonic or a couple of glasses of wine.

We would not have knowingly permitted our children to drink any alcoholic beverage until they reached the legal drinking age. But the mood and the style of the neighborhood were very friendly toward alcohol.

Many years later, as part of an assignment at Hope Haven, Terry wrote:

> *The first time I used alcohol I was 13. I drank 1–2 beers (Colt 45) with my friend Morreen, my boyfriend Bill, and several other friends. Morreen and I stood on our heads to get the effect quicker. I did a cheerleading jump off a 2 1/2-foot wall and forgot to put my legs together to land on my feet and landed squarely on my tailbone, chipping it. I remember before the accident that I was full of energy, laughing and having fun. I think it made it easier to make out with my boyfriend. [November 21, 1994]*

As Laura Blumenfeld observed, this first experience with alcohol became a pattern that held for much of her life: "a moment of soaring, a back-breaking crash."

For the next few years, Terry and her friends would drink on the average four or five beers a week. Sometimes they would try wine or vodka. None of her friends regarded Terry's drinking as beyond the level of typical teenagers at that time. They saw no problem.

Terry and her friends would sometimes get liquor from family bars in the neighborhood. As a precaution, I had placed a padlock on ours. They bypassed this obstacle by removing the screws of the metal fittings to which the padlock was affixed, and after raiding the liquor cabinet they carefully replaced the screws.

Terry, however, encountered more painful difficulties. Bill, the boyfriend whom she mentioned "making out" with, had a different notion of what that activity should include than Terry. She saw it as kissing and embracing. He wanted sexual intercourse, and he pressed Terry incessantly—even intimating in the most anguished terms that he could not live if she rejected his entreaties. He was a bright-eyed, winsome, inwardly troubled teenager, and Terry was in love with him. He was a popular youngster at the time, and it was Terry's misfortune to have won his interest over other aspiring girls in the group. One night after Terry had refused his advances, he went to his home, picked up a rifle, leaned over it, and pulled the trigger. A serious wound in the abdomen nearly cost him his life. After a critical hospitalization, he resumed his pressure on Terry; this time, frightened by his near suicide, she yielded. The result: Terry, age fifteen, became pregnant the very first time she had sexual intercourse.

At the time of her pregnancy, abortion was illegal unless an accredited doctor found that giving birth was a threat to the mother's life. Our family doctor, one of the most distinguished physicians in Washington, was concerned over the impact on Terry's emotional life of trying to deliver a child under the circumstances of the pregnancy. He arranged for a colleague in Florida to perform an abortion. Terry's older sister Susan offered to accompany her, and they made the sad journey to Florida by themselves.

We made these decisions with no consultation or confrontation either with Bill or with his parents, who were going through the pangs of a troubled marriage and divorce. Somehow this seemed like a decision that should center on Terry's welfare; we believed that consulting with her and our trusted doctor, without involving her emotionally unstable boyfriend, was the best way to reach it. I might add that, following his suicide attempt, Bill tried to burn down his parents' home.

An important part of Terry was devastated by the abortion. Her innocence, her fun-loving nature, and her self-confidence were all deeply shaken, first by an unpleasant sexual experience and then by a pregnancy that she feared and yet did not want to terminate. She later told me of these feelings and then added: "I thought that my special relationship with you was over." I never knowingly conveyed such an attitude toward Terry. I never expressed anger, nor did I ever hint at any concern about possible political consequences. But Terry felt shamed and reduced by this episode. In retrospect, I wish I had gone out of my way to reassure her that for me she remained a "special person" whom I both loved and admired despite her teenage mistakes.

During the summer after these events, we were obviously more concerned than we had been about her relationship with Bill and her other social activities. We decided that it would be best for her to leave Washington, so we arranged, with her reluctant cooperation, to enroll her at Lincoln School in Providence, Rhode Island, an excellent Quaker high school for girls.

The tactic failed. Terry was overwhelmed with loneliness and depression—especially after her Bill drifted away from her. The academic performance of this bright and promising girl began to slump, despite the high standards and stimulus of Lincoln School and her parents' frustrated entreaties.

As the year in Providence dragged on through a cold winter, Bill made a few visits, but these soon ended as he became more involved with drug use. When Terry returned to Washington for the summer break, she discovered that Bill and her other friends had added marijuana and pills to their stimulants. Seeking to recover her boyfriend, Terry added pot and amphetamines to her intake—not on a heavy scale, but enough to classify her as a user. Meanwhile, her drinking continued—again, not on a scale heavy enough to indicate to any of her friends that she was doing anything beyond the norm for an adolescent in the 1960s.

Despite her personal difficulties, following her junior year of high school in Providence, Terry learned of a Quaker-run settlement house in Southeast Washington on C Street that was in need of volunteers to assist the resident children—largely black youngsters from impoverished single-parent homes—and offered her services. She moved into the large, shabby old house, devoid of air conditioning and other comforts, and lived there without complaint during the hot, sultry months of July and August 1967. She developed a genuine affection for the children in her care and stayed in contact with some of them long after her service on C Street ended.

We had acquired a comfortable old weekend house on Maryland's Eastern Shore in an area near St. Michaels, which had been named Cedar Point by its previous owners, my House colleague Charles Brown of Missouri and his Missouri friend Jack Kornmeier. The Kornmeiers, who were to become our close friends, owned a large brick weekend house nearby that was part of the Cedar Point complex. They had a beautiful swimming pool, which they kept in immaculate condition. Terry had fallen in love with Cedar Point—especially the Kornmeier swimming pool—and asked me if she could take her settlement children there for a weekend in the country. I okayed the proposal and even nervously agreed to ask Jack and his wife, Patti, if Terry and her children could use their pool. The Kornmeiers graciously agreed.

I shall never forget the joy of that day for Terry and her young charges. Noting, however, the outwardly gracious and yet reserved and nervous demeanor of our friends as they saw their pool commandeered for much of the day, I resolved to build a pool behind our house. Cedar Point, a retreat bordered by woods in the rear and Chesapeake Bay in front, became one of the joys of Terry's life, and remained so for years to come.

The Sunday with her friends from the settlement house remained an inspiring highlight in her memories of Cedar Point. It was Teresa McGovern at her compassionate, imaginative best. From the time she was a child until she died, whenever she had access to a resource that she treasured, her immediate impulse was to share it.

In part, her summer of service at the settlement house was her way of trying to compensate for the terminated pregnancy by helping other children. She had a special sense of compassion and caring for children all of her life. She empathized with their problems, spoke their language, and introduced a sense of delight to their lives.

WITH TERRY AGAIN living at home on Coquelin Terrace, she enrolled for her senior year at the Sandy Springs School at the edge of Washington—a Quaker school from which Ann and Susan had previously graduated. Daily, Eleanor would deliver Terry to Sandy Springs. But, we later learned, frequently a friend would arrive at the school in the afternoon and Terry would skip a class or two to use pot or drink beer.

The cumulative impact of this clandestine schedule of drugs and alcohol reduced the once carefree Terry to a high-strung, sometimes depressed high school senior with little interest in Sandy Springs' academic, cultural, or recreational activities. Since it is probable that Terry had inherited a genetic structure that made her vulnerable to both depression and addiction, the self-indulgent routine that overtook her in the 1960s is all the more regrettable.

I recall one incident when she was scheduled to participate in a rehearsal for the all-school drama and chorus of the annual Christmas program. I was slated to drive her to Sandy Springs that Saturday for this important final rehearsal, but Terry suddenly announced she was not going. "Oh yes you are," I retorted in the most authoritative voice I could muster. In short order, the rhetoric escalated to a test of will and physical strength, with both of us losing our footing, falling in a tangled heap on the kitchen floor, and breaking into laughter as we contemplated our ridiculous posture. I eventually prevailed, but it was a temporary and painfully fleeting victory.

Terry always knew that there was a special affectionate relationship between us and that I very much wanted her to have a
full and satisfying life. The humorous and kidding exchanges
continued, but neither Eleanor nor I was fully aware that our
daughter was setting the stage for serious future problems with
alcohol and drugs. We were frankly baffled by her eroding performance at school and her increasing emotional distress. Neither her academic counselors nor other parents with whom we
conferred were able to offer any helpful insights.

Following graduation from Sandy Springs, Terry decided with
our agreement that perhaps the best place for her to begin her
college days was at our alma mater in South Dakota, Dakota
Wesleyan University, which she remembered fondly from my
teaching years there in the 1950s. She enrolled in the fall of 1967
and seemed to enjoy it. Her transcript for the academic year
1967–68 shows a full academic load with a B average in a solid
range of courses, including composition, sociology, history, economics, education, psychology, American government, and a
course called Art and Civilization, in which she earned an A.

Wesleyan offered several advantages that were appealing to
Terry. It was a small liberal arts school with a warm and friendly
atmosphere. It had a faculty interested in classroom teaching and
in the personal well-being of the students. It was located in a
community filled with pleasant childhood memories for Terry.
And it was fifteen hundred miles from Bill! Terry was particularly fond of Professor Leonard Jennewein, a marvelous history
teacher and a student of Western frontier lore. He was, however,
handicapped by alcoholism—he was a binge drinker who somehow managed to keep it a secret from his students by confining
his drinking to the weekends away from the campus in such
places as Sioux City, Iowa, or Omaha, Nebraska. He died before Terry completed her education at DWU—a death has-
tened by his drinking.

Needless to say, alcohol and drugs had found their way to the campus, if not as spectacularly as in Washington and on the East Coast. Barry Mogin, a pleasant Washington-area friend of Terry's who had experimented with drugs, decided to attend Wesleyan with her. Between the two of them, they occasionally found access to marijuana and beer, but not to the excess that characterized her life on Coquelin Terrace.

Terry's second semester was in the spring of 1968, an election year for me, and I was faced with what appeared to be a tough reelection campaign for the Senate. Terry volunteered to stay in South Dakota and assist in the campaign that summer, which I readily accepted—not only because I welcomed her help and her being with me, but also because it would keep her away from the temptations of Washington.

Since 1965, I had played a leading role in the Senate in trying to end U.S. involvement in the tragically mistaken Vietnam War—a role that had won me a following on the campuses of the nation. A considerable number of college students from across the country thus journeyed to South Dakota ready to enlist in my campaign as unpaid volunteers. One of the best was Molly Shanley, whose father was the highly regarded academic dean of Northwestern University—my graduate school alma mater. Molly and Terry became roommates on the campaign trail and were assigned to a group of two dozen student canvassers who were responsible for working in Rapid City—South Dakota's second-largest city, located in the beautiful Black Hills.

Pot smoking was all too prevalent in 1968 among college students, including some who supported me. But what was different about this collection of student canvassers residing in a Black Hills motel was that it included the daughter of a prominent U.S. senator faced with a hard election—especially among conservative voters in western South Dakota.

Senator Robert Kennedy, then seeking the Democratic presidential nomination on an anti–Vietnam War platform, had won the California and South Dakota primary elections on June 4, and was killed that night in Los Angeles by an assassin's bullet. I was a close friend of his and had talked with him by telephone to give him the voting returns in South Dakota just a few minutes before he was shot. In 1961 and 1962, I had worked at the White House for President John Kennedy, who had appointed me, with his brother's strong support, as the nation's Food for Peace director. Bobby and I had come to know each other well in those years and later as senators in our mutual opposition to the Vietnam War. Indeed, I had urged him to seek the presidency in 1968.

Thus, when he was killed at his moment of triumph, it was a painful blow to me personally as well as to the entire family. Thirty days later, at the urging of his California presidential nominating delegates, I agreed to speak at a memorial luncheon for him in Los Angeles at the hotel where he was shot. I arrived the night before the luncheon and stayed overnight at the home of Louis and Marian Licht, friends of mine who lived on Sunset Boulevard in Beverly Hills. I slept fitfully and awakened early the next morning to the sound of the *Los Angeles Times* hitting the porch below my window. Knowing that I had a scheduled press conference before my noon memorial speech, I wandered out onto the porch to pick up the *Times* and scan the news in preparation for possible questions. There it was on page one: "Senator's Daughter Arrested on Drug Charge." It was Terry.

My blood ran cold—first in anguish over Terry, who was under arrest in Rapid City. This was no minor concern, as I then learned, because the South Dakota legislature had just enacted a law compelling an automatic, mandatory five-year penitentiary sentence for anyone caught in possession of marijuana. Terry was the first arrest under this new law. The prospect of prison for Terry was unbearable. How could it be possible? My ever-struggling daughter who had done so well at Dakota Wesleyan and was so eagerly working on my behalf was now faced with five years in the state penitentiary in Sioux Falls.

Then the second blow hit me. My Senate campaign was probably already over and lost. All those years of cultivating the confidence of the good but conservative people of South Dakota dashed away in one foolish episode. How could I ask South Dakotans who had tolerated my outspoken opposition to a war in which their sons were fighting to support a senator who couldn't even maintain respect for the law in his own family?

I went through the press conference and speech, then caught the next plane to South Dakota to be with Terry as soon as possible. I called Eleanor in Washington and learned that she was already preparing to leave for Rapid City. She had expected me to stay at the hotel where I was speaking and had been unable to reach me during the night. We arrived in Rapid City about the same time and faced the waiting press.

Before leaving Los Angeles I had called two of the most respected lawyers in Rapid City, Wallace McCullen and George Bangs, and they quickly began work on the case. Molly Shanley, who had been apprehended with Terry, since they shared the room where marijuana had been found, was entirely innocent but was still faced with the necessity of proving her innocence. Eleanor and I joined the two girls at the lawyers' offices for a serious and painful conference. The law was clear: a mandatory five-year sentence—no exceptions or qualifying phrases.

We then learned the story of Terry's apprehension. An employee of the motel where our youthful political workers were staying thought she had detected the use of marijuana. She suspected that one of the probable users was candidate McGovern's daughter from Dakota Wesleyan. As a confirmed Republican, she saw her duty: to call the local Republican chairman. He, in turn, clearly saw his duty and called the attorney general—also an active Republican political leader—at the state capital in Pierre, who alerted the Rapid City police. The police then gained the necessary search warrant and went to the motel. No effort was made to search other rooms—only the room of Terry and her roommate. A police search team knocked on their door at midnight. They found a sprig of marijuana in one of the dresser drawers with Terry's personal items and promptly arrested her and her roommate and hauled them off to jail.

Eleanor and I had scarcely arrived in Rapid City before our other children began arriving to show family support. They also came because they sensed a dangerous legal crisis that could mean not only the imprisonment of their sister but the end of their dad's political career. We assembled our family at the comfortable Hisega Lodge, owned and operated by two old friends, Jessie and Carl Sanders. Located on a scenic Black Hills brook several miles north of Rapid City, it was a perfect haven for a family under siege—private, secluded, restful, and friendly. We arrived there deeply troubled, but with each passing day we drew strength from one another and from our lovely surroundings. Jessie, an old Democratic warhorse, had once run unsuccessfully for Congress. She adored our family and asserted almost hourly that somehow everything would come out all right. Despite the concerned reports from our lawyers, which I elicited with frequent nervous telephone calls, we drew consolation from Jessie's energetic assurances. She and Carl prepared delicious meals and took our children fishing, exploring, and swimming. We also explored the Black Hills. No matter what your problems are, they will seem less threatening as you wander through South Dakota's magnificent Black Hills in early July.

And yet every one of us remained deeply troubled by Terry's legal predicament. A long-distance call from my colleague and friend Senator Edward Kennedy was a source of encouragement. He suggested that a Boston lawyer who was an expert in the kind of case that had ensnarled Terry might be willing to advise us. We had confidence in the Rapid City legal team, Bangs and Mc-Cullen, but I have never forgotten Ted Kennedy's thoughtfulness in making that call to South Dakota even as he was overwhelmed with grief over the assassination of his brother Bobby a few days earlier.

Then came a call from our lawyers asking Terry, her roommate, Molly, and Eleanor and me to come to their office to hear about a hopeful development. Carefully researching all aspects of both the law and the procedures leading up to Terry's arrest, they had discovered a crucial error involving the granting of the search warrant. The local judge empowered to authorize such searches had signed a power of attorney to a designated justice of the peace that could be used during the judge's vacation; it was this justice of the peace who had signed the search warrant that led to Terry's arrest. But Bangs and McCullen discovered that the power of attorney had expired at midnight the day before it was used to authorize the search. They were convinced that the court would agree that the search was invalid. When they so moved in court the next day, the judge held in their favor and the case against Terry and her roommate was dismissed. We were all filled with enormous relief.

What was not yet known was the extent of the political damage done to the Senate reelection campaign resulting from the statewide, indeed nationwide, publicity given to the case. But there were a few encouraging signs even before charges against Terry were dropped. I had withdrawn from campaign activities during the crucial week with my family and our lawyers, but our family excursions around the Black Hills had brought us into contact with old friends and other South Dakotans. The reactions of people to Terry's difficulty were encouraging.

One afternoon we were invited to the vast ranch of our friends Lionel and Murman Jensen near Wall, South Dakota—home of the celebrated Wall Drug Store. It is said that Wall Drug sells everything except drugs. Of course, drugs—both prescription and across-the-counter—are sold there. But these sales are dwarfed by the unbelievable array of souvenirs and menu items that include everything from cowboy hats and Indian head-dresses to pancakes and buffalo steaks. The store is advertised on road signs around the globe.

That day of horseback riding and a splendid dinner with the Jensens was refreshing and reassuring to all of us. Terry always found joy and healing in such activities as swimming, horseback riding, and simply meandering around interesting places such as Wall Drug and the Jensen ranch, which stretched out for miles under gorgeous South Dakota blue skies.

I thought that day, as I have many days since, that before entering public life, an aspiring politician should understand and make clear to his family that public service frequently requires private sacrifice. If I were to do it all over again, I would insist on more times of riding with my children, camping with them, engaging in sports with them, teaching them to ski and play tennis, taking leisurely strolls and trips, and just listening to them at home. This is no guarantee of a more secure and happy life for one's children. There are peer pressures and other circumstances beyond the parents' control. But the kind of activities and involvements I have suggested might have been a better way to fortify my children against the heavy pressures and temptations of adolescence, including the Bills of this world. It is, of course, not very profitable to contemplate what might have been, but I nonetheless must pass it on as uninvited advice. I'm pleased to note that my children have been giving my grandchildren such loving attention and enjoyment.

But back to the Jensen ranch. The Jensens were active political allies, highly regarded "solid" citizens known across the state.

Even before the case was dismissed, they had assured us repeatedly that South Dakota voters would not punish us politically for Terry's legal crisis. They reported, too, that many South Dakotans disapproved of the harsh and arbitrary character of the new state marijuana law and of the circumstances of Terry's arrest. I was skeptical about such assurances, but in various ways other South Dakotans were volunteering the same sentiments, including Ted Hustead, the owner of Wall Drug. The superintendent of schools in Rapid City, Dr. Fisher, told me that in his judgment at least a fourth of his students had smoked pot. He assured me that parents across the state were probably saying, "Too bad about the McGoverns. That could have been my kid."

Once Terry had been legally cleared, I began to think about both her future and the necessity of resuming my Senate campaign. There was, however, another unexpected development. My Los Angeles speech to Robert Kennedy's delegates and supporters a week earlier had set off a demonstration of "McGovern for President" cries that startled me and which I could not silence. Other Kennedy supporters from other parts of the country quickly joined in the call. Bill Dougherty, the South Dakota chairman for the Kennedy campaign and a close friend of mine, took these calls seriously and began urging me to do the same— even as I grappled with Terry's legal crisis.

One night during a family dinner at a lodge operated by Carl Burgess, a prominent Black Hills Republican and former speaker of the state legislature, I sheepishly mentioned to Carl that I was being urged to announce for the presidency and asked for his opinion. Without a word he took out his checkbook and wrote me a $5,000 check made out to "The McGovern for President Committee." I could easily have assumed that this was his method of getting me out of the Senate campaign in South Dakota! But I sensed that despite our party differences, he was a genuine admirer and friend and saw nothing ridiculous at all in such a presidential bid. His reaction prompted me to at least keep the possibility in the back of my mind.

A few days later, Eleanor and I left with Congressman John Brademas of Indiana as Congressional invitees to the World Council of Churches meeting in Uppsala, Sweden. It was a good opportunity to get out from under the pressure of both state and national politics and to recover from the trauma of Terry's near imprisonment. But when we landed in London, Morley Safer of CBS was waiting and asked whether I would announce a presidential candidacy in order to lead the Kennedy delegates to the national nominating convention in Chicago. I avoided comment, and Eleanor and I continued on to the Uppsala conference for a week with church delegates from all over the world. By the time we returned to Washington, Robert Kennedy's key staff members and consultants were waiting for me. A few days later, after winning the blessings of my wife and children, I agreed to announce for the presidency.

It was a highly risky political move for a junior South Dakota senator in the middle of his first campaign for reelection to the Senate. But, as usual, my family threw themselves into the effort. I had observed to Eleanor late one night in the Black Hills that if the country was so mixed up that we were fighting a foolish and hopeless war in Vietnam while American kids were increasingly involved in drugs at home and increasingly hostile toward their government, maybe I should move into the presidential forum with a different message. I wanted to get American forces out of Vietnam immediately and begin addressing the neglected needs of American society. It was my hope that a national campaign based on candor and common sense could help restore the credibility of our government. It pleased me that Terry and my other children were ready to enlist in this brief effort aimed at influencing the Democratic convention in Chicago.

I recall Terry intently observing this highly emotional gathering with rioting in the Chicago streets and violent clashes between the police and the antiwar supporters of McCarthy and, formerly, Kennedy. The protesting young Americans were not happy with either the police tactics in the streets or the presidential nominating process leading up to the convention. Terry, just turned nineteen, was experiencing her first national political convention—perhaps the most turbulent one in American history—and her father was a key participant. She and my other children tasted in concentrated form that week the whole range of political competition, national division, police excesses, overwrought protest, and bitter political combat. It was not a very pleasant introduction to national convention experience, but it was fiercely exciting, sometimes exhilarating and sometimes terrifying.

Our Washington neighbor and friend Hubert Humphrey had been selected by President Lyndon Johnson as his vice presidential running mate in 1964. He was challenged for the presidential nomination in 1968 by Senator Eugene McCarthy and Senator Robert Kennedy because of his support for Johnson's continuance of the Vietnam War. My agreement to lead the Kennedy delegates to the Chicago convention was based on the same consideration. By that time all of the presidential nominating delegates had been selected and Humphrey, with Johnson's backing, had the nomination virtually locked up. In effect, the national convention was a battle over the Vietnam War. Once Humphrey's nomination was decided by the convention, I quickly backed him in the general election against the GOP nominee—former Vice President Richard Nixon—despite my opposition to the Vietnam policy of both presidential nominees. I preferred Humphrey over Nixon because of their contrasting records on domestic questions and because of Humphrey's valiant fight over the years for civil rights. But, dismayed by the Johnson-Humphrey support for the Vietnam War and by what appeared to be a stacked nominating procedure, many of the McCarthy-Kennedy supporters never joined the Humphrey battle with Nixon after the bitter Chicago experience.

Still shaken by her arrest and near imprisonment in South Dakota, Terry stayed close to her mother during those hectic days in Chicago and tried to make sense of the unfolding events. It was a most effective way to recover from her self-inflicted trauma in Rapid City, as there was no time to dwell on one's personal problems during the Chicago convention of '68. The McGovern family came across well in that first brief presidential foray and then headed to South Dakota to resume the Senate race.

We were uncertain what the reaction in South Dakota would be to the combination of Terry's highly publicized case and my presidential side trip to Chicago. But that Senate race turned out to be the easiest and most decisive win I ever scored in South Dakota. The Democrats responded with a solid and enthusiastic rallying around my candidacy and with great sympathy and support for our family. And so did an unprecedented number of Republicans. Day after day as I moved across the state, people would stop me to say, "I'm a Republican, but I didn't like that move against your daughter," or "You were the class act at that Democratic convention in Chicago," or "I thought you were wrong when you started warning against Vietnam years ago, but I'm now with you all the way." All in all, it was a highly gratifying reelection campaign. I've been grateful to South Dakota voters many times, but at no time more than in 1968. The victory in South Dakota, assuring me another six years in the U.S. Senate, combined with the heart-stirring, head-filling presidential foray in Chicago, left dreams in my head of a possible future road to the White House. Perhaps with some degree of rationalization, I even thought such a venture might give a new and constructive focus to my children, including, especially, troubled Terry.

*The 1972 New York State presidential primary victory. I am flanked by
Terry and Eleanor, with Terry's cousin Carol Brady behind us.*

F O U R

"Teresa was truly a good person."

E MBARRASSED BY HER Rapid City marijuana arrest, Terry decided not to return to Dakota Wesleyan that fall. She chose instead to pursue her interest in psychology by enrolling at Clark University in Worcester, Massachusetts—a school with a strong tradition in that field, the only American university ever to host Sigmund Freud as a lecturer. She had shown some signs of anxiety and depression early that fall, but Eleanor and I believed that the Clark experience might be helpful to her.

On election night that fall, we were able to celebrate the biggest victory margin in my Senate career. Terry was especially delighted with the outcome because it signaled that there was no lasting political damage from her arrest. Not until after her death did I learn of a dangerously destructive incident that Terry had been involved in on the eve of the 1968 voting. During my years representing South Dakota in the Congress, I had developed a tradition of gathering the family for an informal discussion that went out across the state on live television the night before each election. Terry had returned from Clark for this event. I noticed that she was nervous; unknown to me, she was under the influence of a heavy dose of LSD.

She confided in Steve, and he advised her to stay as calm as possible and go forward with the TV appearance. He also gave special attention to her during the seventy-mile drive from our home in Mitchell to the Sioux Falls TV studio. Terry kept quiet during the telecast except for one brief comment and managed to conceal her confused state.

Her brother had tried to encourage her on the ride back to Mitchell that night, whispering to her that her distraught mind would clear in the morning. Such was not the case, and when she returned to Clark shortly after the election she was terrified by her depressed emotional state. From that point on, her academic performance collapsed and she dropped out of Clark at midterm, returning to our home in Washington.

One Sunday evening shortly thereafter, when Terry, Eleanor, and I were driving back to Washington after a pleasant weekend at Cedar Point, Terry began to sob.

"I can't stand what is happening to me," she said. "I'm so discouraged and sad about my life that I don't believe I can keep going."

Without knowing the extent of her LSD and alcohol intake, we had previously become aware of her deepening sadness. The next day we sought out knowledgeable friends for advice.

One of these was Joe Floyd, South Dakota's major television executive and a close family friend. We knew that Joe had been treated occasionally for clinical depression at the University of Virginia Psychiatric Center in Charlottesville. At Joe's suggestion, we telephoned his doctor, Wilfred Abse, and arranged to bring Terry in after Christmas for an evaluation.

Early in January, Terry, Eleanor, and I drove to Charlottesville. Except for a few brief interludes, Terry remained there for the next five years for what proved to be one of the happiest and most constructive periods of her life. During all but the first six months she had daily one-hour sessions with a distinguished psychoanalyst, Dr. Vamik Volkan—a man whom she came to trust and for whom she had growing admiration and affection.

She had her own apartment during most of this time, worked part-time as an admissions aide at the university hospital, and took courses part-time at the university. She also developed a warm friendship that became a delightful lengthy romance with a student at UVA.

Terry's first six months in Charlottesville, however, were neither pleasant nor easy. The doctors who examined and interrogated her were so alarmed by the depth of her depression that they placed her in a locked ward of the psychiatric center. They believed that she was a threat to herself and needed both constant surveillance and extensive treatment. Eleanor and I were shocked by this diagnosis and by what seemed like a hasty decision that Terry should immediately be committed for intensive treatment. We decided, nonetheless, to accept the judgment of the university medical professionals.

When we had kissed Terry goodbye and heard the heavy door shut, its automatic lock clicking firmly into place, it was heartbreaking to look back through the glass at the forlorn little figure looking out at us, her eyes filled with tears. She wanly waved goodbye to us from the soundproof ward, which was in a sense an imprisonment. That farewell image stayed in my mind all the way back to Washington and returned to me many times in the months ahead.

There was no alcohol or drug use during this six-month confinement until the last month, when a boyfriend in Washington, Barry Mogin, smuggled in a small amount of marijuana and LSD. Terry talked to Barry about the pain of her depression while she was hospitalized. She also shared with him her conclusion that the only way out of her misery was suicide. Telling him that she was determined to take that way out, she begged him to smuggle in a supply of sleeping pills, which she planned to swallow in one deadly gulp. She was then nineteen.

Barry concluded that with or without his cooperation, Terry would find a way to end her life. He agonized over this dilemma and finally came up with a ruse that probably saved her life. Promising to secure the pills on his return to Washington, he instead filled two dozen capsules with flour and a few crushed aspirins and passed them to Terry on his next visit.

Shortly thereafter, she escaped from the hospital, bought a pint of vodka, rented a cheap room, washed down the capsules with the vodka, and lay down to die.

Instead, she awakened a few hours later with a hangover. She walked out into the sunshine with the birds chirping on a beautiful spring day and thanked God that she was still alive. To the best of my knowledge, this was her only serious suicide attempt. She never ceased to thank Barry for his lifesaving ingenuity. And she began progressing in the battle with depression.

When she turned twenty in June 1969, and was apparently stabilized following the aborted suicide attempt, her hospital confinement was ended and she moved into a small apartment on Buckingham Circle near the university. That apartment was a joy to her—especially after half a year of confinement in the psychiatric ward. Throughout her life, Terry never failed to furnish and arrange her apartments as tastefully and as lovingly as possible given the limitations of illness and her always pinched budget. Each picture had to be hung exactly in the appropriate place. Her books had to be arranged carefully on shelves she might make herself. Her knickknacks had to be lovingly displayed, and whenever the season permitted, she had fresh or potted flowers. Usually she would purchase a parakeet, which then resided in an old green cage we had given her. She would work long hours teaching the bird to talk. The bird's reward would be freedom to fly and hop around the apartment outside the cage for a period each day. Each bird that she ever owned had a special name and a special place in her life.

Once her Charlottesville apartment was in order in the summer of 1969, she started daily psychoanalysis with Dr. Volkan, which extended over the next four and a half years. She participated in these sessions faithfully, worked at her part-time job successfully, and was a serious part-time student at the university, taking courses in public speaking, American history, Russian history, ecology, astronomy, art, criminology, and psychology. The University of Virginia had only recently opened its doors to women students, and it was difficult for out-of-state residents to gain admission, especially women. Terry resolved this problem by taking her coursework at the more accessible campus at Madison, Virginia—thirty miles from Charlottesville—where the state university operated a center suitable for part-time adult students wishing to supplement their education. She had hoped that this considerable effort in daily driving and study at the Madison campus would eventually open the way for admission to the main university campus in Charlottesville—a hope that did not materialize, to her deep disappointment.

Terry loved reading good novels, and she became conversant with the best American and British works. She always maintained a collection of books on the makeshift shelves of her homes throughout her life, and she discussed them with intelligence and perception.

She also became an accomplished writer, an effective campaign speaker, and a follower of the theater and the arts. She had a first-rate mind despite the frequent clouding of alcohol. She sometimes imagined that she was not as intelligent as her brother or sisters, but this stemmed from her alcohol-induced loss of self-esteem, not from mental limitations.

Dr. Volkan probably came to know more about her inner life, her personality, her character, and her weaknesses and strengths than any other person. When Eleanor and I went to visit him following Terry's death, he manifested genuine grief. His professional ethics prevented him from revealing much about the hundreds of counseling sessions he had with Terry, but he said: "I want to emphasize one fact. Teresa was truly a good person, an unusually good person. I came to know her very well and she was a notably good person."

Unfortunately, once released from the hospital Terry accompanied her psychiatric counseling with a daily average intake during those years that she later estimated to be "5–6 beers daily or 3–4 shots of hard liquor, or a bottle of wine."

In her journal in October 1989 she recorded her lifetime drinking habits year by year:

TERRY'S OWN ALCOHOL HISTORY AS SHE REMEMBERS IT
JOURNAL, OCTOBER 1989

1965 age 16   *Alcohol—very occasionally, 5 or 6 times a year*
                     Amphetamines—3 or 4 times

1966 age 17   *Marijuana—3 or 4 times a week*
                     Barbiturates—3 or 4 times a year
                     Amphetamines—10–15 times

1967 age 18   *Marijuana—daily for about 2 months*
                     Amphetamines—daily for a week
                     Alcohol—2 to 3 beers every other weekend
                     LSD—2 to 3 times a year

1968 age 19   *LSD—3 to 4 times a week for about 2 months*
                     Alcohol—very rarely—approximately 3 or 4 times that year
                     Hospitalized Jan. '69 (age 19) for 6 mos., UVA
                     No alcohol or drug use until last month—LSD once; pot once

1969 age 20 Daily drinking—3–4 beers or equivalent in other kinds
of alcohol
LSD—5 to 6 times that year
1969–79 ages 20–30 Average 5–6 beers daily or 3–4 shots of hard
liquor, or a bottle of wine
1970 age 21 Daily drinking
1971 age 22   "   "
1972 age 23   "   "   } Pot, very sporadic
1973 age 24   "   "
1974 age 25   "   "
1975 age 26   "   "   Pot, once a week
1976 age 27   "   "
1977 age 28   "   "   } Amphetamines at midterms
1978 age 29   "   "   } and final exams
1979 age 30   "   "

To complete the record, at age thirty-one, in 1980, Terry began an eight-year period of sobriety that ended in 1988 when she was thirty-nine. After a relapse of two or three months, she achieved another year of sobriety. Then came a relapse in early 1990, after her fortieth birthday. The drinking then continued until her death in 1994, except for many brief periods of detoxification and several recovery treatments of a month or so.

When Terry was going through psychoanalysis in the years 1969–73, the view of most psychiatrists, including those at the University of Virginia, was that heavy drinking or drug abuse was not likely the central issue for their patients. The problem as they saw it—especially the Freudian psychiatrists—was psychological, stemming from emotional damage most likely incurred in childhood. If a patient was too dependent on alcohol or other drugs, it was because of faulty family relationships, or unhealthy child-rearing procedures, or deep-seated sexual maladjustments. The notion that alcoholism might be the major cause of the patient's depression, anxiety, and low self-esteem was alien to most psychiatrists. Alcohol abuse was a symptom, not a cause, of emotional illness, they believed.

To this day, practicing medical doctors, psychiatrists, and specialists in alcoholism dispute the relative importance of physiological versus psychological factors as a basis for alcoholism. However, there is a growing consensus, which I share, that the basic cause of the disease is a physiological genetic structure inherited at birth. But I do not rule out Dr. Volkan's diagnosis of Terry. Let me paraphrase the substance of his conclusions:

We don't know for certain what causes vulnerability to alcohol leading to alcoholism, Dr. Volkan said, but Teresa was not suffering from alcoholism in any serious or obvious way in this period, 1969–73. Her basic problem was depression and related psychological conflicts.

Alcoholism probably stems from both physiological and psychological factors, Dr. Volkan believes. Teresa's central core composed of physiological and psychological ingredients was probably agitated and weakened by LSD trips in her teen years, although there were only a few of them for brief periods of time and we really don't know what lasting effect LSD has. This is still speculative. But Teresa feared LSD as a bad experience that had disrupted her life and left her in a weakened condition.

Dr. Volkan believes that Terry "progressed very well" in the years that he worked with her and that she was essentially happy and enthusiastic about her life and her personal growth in this period. He concluded that when she would occasionally express anger or resentment toward her parents or siblings, "this was her way of verbalizing her own contradictions and conflicts. She deeply loved all of you."

Dr. Volkan was gratified with Terry's steady development over this five-year period—as was she. Occasionally after she left Charlottesville, she would telephone him to discuss a problem, and she returned for one additional session a decade later that "went very well." He then lost contact with her, but by coincidence was lecturing to a group of psychiatrists in Milwaukee the day Terry died.

"I was terribly shocked and saddened to read of her death in the *Milwaukee Journal*," Dr. Volkan told us. His eyes glistening, he said softly, "How I wish that she and I had talked that day."

When Eleanor and I expressed our regrets that we had distanced ourselves from Terry in what turned out to be the last months of her life, Dr. Volkan replied: "There is another way of looking at this. You paid her the honor of encouraging her to become an independent person. She paid you the honor of not burdening you with the knowledge of how threatening her illness had become. You and she were showing your love for each other in a mature way."

IN MARCH 1971, Jeff Ferrill arrived in Charlottesville after nearly three years of service in the U.S. Army. He began working twelve to fifteen hours daily, six days a week, as a driver of taxis, buses, and ambulances; he was trying to earn enough money to attend the University of Virginia. Late one night in early April, he stopped by a party at the Raleigh Court apartments on University Circle. Having worked a long day, he was not in a very festive mood, but he noticed "an attractive girl sitting alone watching television. I went over and introduced myself and talked with her awhile about old movies. We then sat and watched the rest of *The List of Adrian Messenger*. The girl's name was Terry McGovern."

Over the next several weeks, Terry and Jeff talked frequently on the telephone and had several informal dates. "The first few months with Terry were enjoyable," Jeff later wrote. "Our dates usually consisted of a movie and dinner at a local Chinese restaurant, local pub (Poe's or the Mousetrap), or at Terry's apartment at 113 West Buckingham Circle. On weekend afternoons we would take a drive along the Skyline Drive in the Blue Ridge Mountains or go swimming in Via's Lake, a small freshwater lake about twenty minutes from Charlottesville near Free Union, Virginia.

"During those first few months, Terry talked very little about her family or herself. I can remember feeling that while Terry had gotten to know me fairly well, I knew little about her. Then one morning we met for breakfast at the College Inn near the UVA Corner. Terry suddenly started telling me why she was in Charlottesville; about her overdoses of drugs; attempted suicide; her hospitalization in the UVA psychiatric ward; her psychoanalysis; her family. I think she expected me to get up, leave, and never see her again. Instead, we spent the rest of the day together talking about ourselves and really enjoying the closeness we were beginning to feel."

Jeff Ferrill's father, a military man, had wanted his son to enroll in one of the service academies. He regarded the University of Virginia as too much of a "social school" and informed Jeff that his decision to go there meant that he was primarily on his own financially. Thus the reason for Jeff's long working hours combined with a full course load. He was a strong person, both physically and intellectually, and combined these strengths with a delightful personality and a quiet sense of humor. I liked him on first meeting, and that liking and admiration grew with the passing of time. He was to become an important man in Terry's life.

IN JANUARY 1971, after extensive consultation with my family, staff members, and key backers, including the man who was to become my campaign finance chairman, Henry Kimelman, I announced my candidacy for the Democratic presidential nomination.

It was clear that a bid for the nomination by a junior senator from a sparsely populated state such as South Dakota would be a bruising, uphill battle. My children sometimes worried about another factor. Having witnessed the assassinations of John Kennedy, Robert Kennedy, and Martin Luther King, they feared that I might be shot by some deranged person or right-wing extremist who would kill me rather than see me become President.

"I wanted to see you win the nomination, but I also really feared it," Terry told me after the election. "It was sad to see you lose to Nixon, but in a way I'm glad you lost. I don't think you would have been allowed to reach the White House."

But when I formally entered the presidential nominating battle in early 1971, Terry and my other children began to think about how they could help. "I think Terry felt that by successfully campaigning for her dad, she could erase some of the pain she felt she had caused her family in the past," Jeff Ferrill wrote.

That summer, she left her job and her classes and began to travel and speak on my behalf in the primary election states. With summer school behind him, Jeff joined Terry in August at her invitation for campaign appearances in Massachusetts, New York, Wisconsin, and California. In these important primary states—all of which I won—Terry would frequently team up with Hollywood stars and other entertainment celebrities working for my nomination. She came to know Candice Bergen, Warren Beatty, Shirley MacLaine, Paul Newman, Jack Nicholson, Dennis Weaver, Julie Christie, Leonard Nimoy, and Marlo Thomas, as well as such musicians as Henry Mancini, Andy Williams, Dionne Warwick, Carole King, James Taylor, Barbra Streisand, and Peter Yarrow, Paul Stookey, and Mary Travers. Usually one of them would say a few words on my behalf and then Terry or one of my other children would speak. Terry became increasingly confident and effective as a campaigner.

She was on hand for the turbulent Miami convention when I was nominated in July 1972. Then from late August until the November election she threw herself into the general election campaign. Jeff Ferrill had graduated from the university in August 1972 and gone to work for a Charlottesville law firm. His boss was a strong supporter of mine and granted him leave to join the campaign with Terry. He recalls those days:

I was always very proud of the way Terry would stand up before a crowd and give a spontaneous pep talk. She would usually capture everyone's attention by telling a little joke and then quickly move into telling them why they should vote for her dad. I suppose I admired her all the more because I knew how nervous she was. She especially suffered from stage fright in front of large crowds. She would ask me to position myself in the center front of the crowd where she could easily see me. She hardly ever noticed me, but always said that as long as she knew I was there she would be okay. I suspect that even when I wasn't around, Terry was fine.

Two trips stand out in my memory: one a lengthy car caravan through southern California and a "Grassroots Grasshopper" van tour through central Texas. Both trips lasted about a week. We were accompanied by prominent politicians or their spouses and several movie stars (or "sparklies," as Terry called them). We usually started very early and campaigned late. We stayed in small motels or at supporters' homes along the way. Terry's stamina was incredible; she always was willing to keep going no matter the hour. I think we both matured and gained more self-confidence during these trips.

I especially remember spending two nights at the home of John Henry Faulk and Liz Faulk in Austin, Texas. Their home was located in the hills overlooking the city. Although tired after a long day on the road, we stayed up late with the Faulks talking about politics and "life." Terry and John Henry really hit it off. Later, John Henry wrote of Terry as "one of those rare folk who make this earth a safer, happier place to dwell for us all, and those yet to come." I can think of no better description of Terry during those days.

Eleanor and I had little opportunity to observe Terry's campaign appearances, since each member of the family had his or her own campaign agenda across the nation. But two events stand out in my memory. One rare time when Eleanor and I shared the same hotel room, we awakened in the morning to NBC's *Today* show. There were our daughters—Ann, Susan, and Terry—being interviewed by Barbara Walters and Hugh Downs. They had been given no briefing by me or any of the campaign staff. Indeed, Eleanor and my children were seldom briefed before public appearances. I thought they were magnificent that morning as all three of them fluently answered questions about both the campaign strategy and the great national issues—why the United States should get out of Vietnam, why the tax and welfare systems should be reformed, why George McGovern should be elected President. Eleanor and I did a little dance of delight over the skill, intelligence, and common sense of our daughters. And they all looked beautiful.

One morning, we discovered Terry's newfound prowess had been ratified by no less an authority than *The New York Times.* There was an unexpected story headlined "A New Star Is Born." It was about Terry's campaigning with the Grassroots Grasshopper. The headline told it all—Terry was winning over audiences and gaining votes for her dad in tough political territory, in the Deep South and other places that I seldom if ever visited that fall.

Pat Borden, a reporter for *The Charlotte Observer*, devoted her entire account of the Grasshopper visit to Charlotte on Friday, October 20, 1972, to Terry:

> It was just after eight o'clock Friday morning and Terry McGovern was sitting among several young women supporters before going into the convention hall of the White House Inn to join the other speakers traveling on the Grasshopper Special.

The event was a breakfast, honoring Terry and the others who had come to earn votes for the McGovern-Shriver ticket.

It came on the heels of a four-hour sleep for Terry, who had fallen into bed at 3:00 A.M., forty-five minutes after the Special had rolled into town from the Virginia coast.

"This is our third day on the bus," she said in a soft voice that was nearly swallowed up by the overriding hum of the crowd lined up for the buffet breakfast. "But I've been actively campaigning for the past five weeks."

The past four years have been fraught with growing pains for Terry, now twenty-three and between schools while campaigning for her father.

In 1968, she was charged with the possession of marijuana, no small blow to either her father's career or the family unit. The charges were dropped, but the attendant publicity made the event no less of an ordeal.

It did bring the McGoverns' attention sharply to the plight of their middle child, one of five.

"I've had to dig down deep in myself to get self-confidence," she said, recalling the past few years. "The first speech I had to give, I didn't think I'd live through it.

"As a middle child, I've always been either too old or too young. My parents said I was a show-off as a child, but I don't think anyone ever 'shows off' except to get attention."

Asked to compare what her public image would be should George McGovern be elected, as compared to that of Tricia Nixon Cox, Terry didn't hesitate.

"I feel I would represent young people a little more than she has. I think she has stereotyped herself to be like her father, to be remote and unapproachable. Maybe that's what she wanted, I don't know.

"Personally, I wouldn't want to live in the White House, anyway, but that's beside the point."

When it came her turn to speak, it was evident that she had left fear behind, even though she followed the eloquence of

Cissy Farenthold and Myrlie Evers, widow of civil rights leader Medgar Evers.

Terry has not yet gained force or a fine articulation. Yet, she was the representation of youth that she had spoken of, as she used the same quiet, even voice she uses in conversation.

It was over in a matter of moments, the facing of blinding glare and bristling microphones, and she joined the others as they moved swiftly through the parted crowd back to the waiting Grasshopper Special.

The remarks that Terry gave at the Charlotte breakfast were recorded by another local reporter, Kay Tucker of the *Charlotte News*. Taking note of the comments by certain politicians and political columnists to the effect that George McGovern was "too nice a guy" for the rough-and-tumble battle required to reach the presidency, Terry told the crowd that "just because a man has decency doesn't mean he can't be elected to the highest office in the country.

"My father is not a great man but the kinds of things he believes in are great," she said.

I like that remark because it brings back so many memories of Terry's facial expressions when she was listening to me speak to audiences over the years. She usually manifested approval and pride, combined with a slight smile that seemed to say: "You sound great, but don't forget, I know that you have the same human frailties and sins as the rest of us." She was right about that: none of my children ever bought the notion that their dad was "too good" to be President.

There were several factors that contributed to the landslide defeat of 1972. Terry, through no fault of hers, was indirectly involved in one of those factors—the so-called Eagleton affair. When I selected Missouri Senator Tom Eagleton as my vice presidential running mate, any chance of an upset over the entrenched President Richard Nixon was terminated. Eagleton was a talented, attractive young senator whose selection as my running mate was warmly praised by my Senate colleagues, including majority leader Mike Mansfield, Walter Mondale, Edward Kennedy, and Gaylord Nelson.

What none of us knew, despite discussions with the leading politicians and political journalists of Missouri—and of course with Eagleton—was that he had been secretly suffering for years from clinical depression alternating with emotional highs. Hospitalizations for this illness had included extensive electric shock therapy, which was used before the drug lithium came into medical usage.

When the Senator's medical record was leaked to two reporters, I had to move quickly to discover the facts and to state my position on the issue.

Most of my advisers believed from the outset that this revelation was a political disaster that could only be contained by immediately dropping my chosen running mate and selecting a replacement. But as Eleanor and I listened to Tom's anguished discussion of the matter a week after his selection, we decided to stay with him.

We reacted as we did in considerable part because Terry had been suffering from a clinical depression not unlike Tom Eagleton's. Despite our concern with Tom's problem and its impact on the national campaign and the subsequent problems that could arise if he became Vice President, I could not in effect punish him for being a victim of depression. Doubtless, my decision carried more compassion than realism. I announced to the press that I believed Senator Eagleton's emotional problems were then under control and that I was behind him "a thousand percent." The reaction of my campaign workers, fund-raisers, and many others across the country was so negative that it threatened to cripple the campaign. Beyond this, a number of distinguished psychiatrists advised me that I must reverse my decision in the interest of the nation.

Reluctantly, I asked Senator Eagleton to step down. Immediately and ceaselessly, the national press and my political opponents accused me of not being able to hold to my convictions. Thus I suffered from a double political setback: the negative reaction to my initial decision to stay with Eagleton and the secondary impact of my reversal of this decision, which was blown out of proportion. I was hurt more during the campaign by the Eagleton affair than Nixon was by the Watergate scandals, which forced his resignation from office shortly after the election. His Vice President, Spiro Agnew, also resigned his office to avoid legal prosecution and possible imprisonment for felonious conduct.

Terry followed all of this with special insight and concern based on her personal experiences. She supported my initial decision to stay with Senator Eagleton, but she was also convinced within a week that the decision had to be reversed. Her explanation to Cissy Farenthold, the recent Democratic candidate for the governorship of Texas with whom Terry campaigned, was "totally convincing," Ms. Farenthold told me.

It would, of course, be ridiculous to blame Terry for the decision on Eagleton or to suggest that this issue was the key factor in the Nixon landslide. We were in all probability out of the race before it started when Governor George Wallace was shot during the Maryland primary and was unable to mount his intended independent presidential campaign as he had done in 1968, when he did not have nearly the national political strength he had in 1972. Wallace would have taken much of the South and millions of other voters away from Nixon had he not fallen victim to a would-be assassin. This would have opened the way for me to carry a number of states and possibly even win the election.

Another troublesome factor was that organized labor—under the late George Meany—declined to support my candidacy, in considerable part because of my opposition to the Vietnam War and my identification with reforms in the presidential-nomination process. Meany saw these reforms as a threat to special consideration for organized labor within the Democratic Party.

Beyond this, the delivery of my acceptance speech after 2 A.M. cost me the best opportunity of the campaign to reach a national audience.

Terry was keenly aware of these costly political factors, which were largely beyond our control. She, like the rest of my family, was crushed by the landslide Nixon victory—one that has been equaled only once since then: President Ronald Reagan's defeat of Walter Mondale in 1984 in every state of the union except Minnesota.

"WHEN TERRY RETURNED to Charlottesville, I remember her as being very, very quiet for long periods of time," Jeff Ferrill recalls. Yet, the campaign experience seemed to give her new insights into human behavior, including her own. She was proud of what she had done in the campaign, despite our discouraging numerical defeat.

Terry's drinking never seemed to be a problem during my campaign. But there were quiet signs that it was becoming a larger issue. Jeff recalls that during his early times with Terry, from the spring of 1971 through the early spring primary elections a year later, they "would drink beer or wine at dinner, but I recall no unusual or excessive abuse by Terry." After Jeff had a falling-out with his landlord and Terry had returned to Charlottesville for several months between her primary and general election campaigning, he moved into Terry's apartment on Buckingham Circle.

"Terry was having an intense and often turbulent period in her analysis," Jeff recalled. "She was also torn between feeling happy and proud at the outcome of the primary campaign but at the same time she worried about the likelihood of her family constantly being under public scrutiny."

During this time, Jeff and Terry began making weekend trips to our Chesapeake Bay house at Cedar Point. They cherished those weekends by themselves.

"Terry so loved Cedar Point," Jeff wrote. "Besides the natural beauty of the Maryland Eastern Shore, I think Terry liked the virtual isolation of the location. She could totally relax in a non-threatening environment. We would take long bike rides or walks together, sun by the pool, or I would mow the grass and putter around the yard while Terry would study or read." Sometimes they would drive to the Crab Claw Restaurant at St. Michaels or ride the Tred Avon ferry for dinner at the Oxford Inn.

Jeff also recalls, however, that he and Terry were beginning to have arguments over her increasing consumption of beer. In the months they lived together at Terry's apartment in Charlottesville, Jeff would usually study in the evenings while Terry was either engrossed in her studies, reading, or watching a movie on television. Sometimes she would go through twelve "pony" bottles of Rolling Rock beer while absorbed in a movie. She did not take kindly to Jeff's questions about her drinking. Once she broke into tears, imploring him: "Why am I so messed up?" Such times were rare, but after the election when the trips to Cedar Point resumed, Jeff recalls the arguments with Terry over her drinking escalated.

On the return three-and-a-half-hour trip from Cedar Point to Charlottesville, Terry "liked to take a jug of wine to drink on the return trip. . . . In retrospect, I suppose this was possibly an early indication of the problems Terry would have for the rest of her life."

Still, there was no doubt Jeff and Terry had grown very close. One summer afternoon in 1973, while they were in the pool at Cedar Point, Jeff asked Terry if she would marry him. Terry replied that she couldn't consider that until she had completed her college degree and had her life in better order. She very much wanted to gain admission to the University of Virginia in Charlottesville to complete her education, but she could not surmount the entrance requirements—tough for all students, especially out-of-state women. This was a keen disappointment for Terry and, perhaps, an ill-fated turning point in her life. She had found life in the university community there more supportive and enjoyable than any other setting. Jeff, of course, was part of this pleasant way of life. Terry reluctantly left Charlottesville to enroll at Clark University, hoping to do well enough there to gain later admission to the University of Virginia.

Although Jeff frequently visited Terry at Clark, they missed each other painfully during that academic year, 1973–74. Jeff had rented a three-bedroom cottage located on Richland Farms near Charlottesville. Terry had left her furniture, her car, her dog, Brae, and her cat, George, with Jeff to "guarantee my return." She spent the summer of 1974 with Jeff, again trying for admission to the University of Virginia and again failing.

With several longtime friends and former colleagues at UVA, I could have helped Terry gain admission to the Charlottesville school. She, however, wanted to be accepted on her own merits—not by political pull. My own view at the time was that she had publicly demonstrated enough intelligence and personality in the recent presidential campaign to have won the approval of a fair-minded admissions official.

She was not enthusiastic about returning to Clark in the fall of 1974, partly because of its high costs. Instead, she decided to complete her degree at the University of South Dakota at Vermillion, a pleasant small town in the southeast corner of the state near the Missouri River. For Terry and Jeff, the chief drawback was the distance from Charlottesville.

Terry's older sister Ann had spent two happy and productive years at USD. Terry's friend Nikki Abourezk, the daughter of my Senate colleague from South Dakota, James Abourezk, was also a student there. Eleanor and I thought it would be the kind of low-pressure school that would be good for Terry.

Terry and Nikki shared an apartment in Vermillion beginning with the fall semester of 1974. As Terry headed toward graduation in 1976, with a major in psychology, they became the closest of friends. But during this two-year period, Terry's drinking began to dominate her life.

The University of South Dakota was then a place where heavy drinking and pot smoking were common, and Terry steadily increased her intake of alcohol with some limited use of marijuana and amphetamines. She was the "life of the party"—and there were many weekend parties at USD.

Her brother, Steve, enrolled at USD in January 1975 and shared quarters with Terry and Nikki, first in an uncomfortable small apartment and then on the second floor of a house. The bottom floor was occupied by three other female students, including Terry's cousin Carol Brady. Steve noted that they were all drinking too much. He became worried about Terry, especially when one Sunday with no liquor in the house and the bars closed, Terry went to the kitchen and drank all of the cooking extracts that had any alcoholic content.

"In those days, we thought that alcoholism was something that happened to someone's dad or uncle or grandfather. Students might drink too much—but alcoholism, no way," Steve later recalled. Terry just needed to watch it and be a little more temperate, he thought.

Nikki recalls that "everyone was drinking in those days—plus smoking pot and using speed. I was heavier in the drug department than Terry. Furthermore, she studied every night during the week and confined her drinking to the weekends. During the two years I either lived with her or associated with her at USD, I never thought of her as a 'problem drinker.' She may have been on the road to alcoholism, but she drank no more than the rest of us." Nikki was probably right about that. The difference was that Terry was vulnerable to addiction; Nikki was not.

Later that spring, Steve came to know the student editor of the USD newspaper, the *Volante,* a quiet, thoughtful student from Kansas by the name of Bob Martin. Majoring in photo-journalism, Steve was given assignments with the *Volante,* and he and Bob became friends. This soon led to Bob's meeting Terry and Nikki, whom he wanted to interview for the *Volante* as the daughters of South Dakota's two U.S. senators and roommates at the state's university. Bob and Terry began dating shortly thereafter, and by the end of the summer they had decided to look for a place where they could live together. Terry had enrolled for the 1975 summer session but dropped out on July 26 after her class attendance and academic performance had deteriorated. Her drinking had increased during the summer. Eleanor and I were disappointed and concerned about Terry's academic decline, but we did not associate it with excessive drinking, which in retrospect seems puzzling.

One night that summer, Nikki and Terry heard a loud noise. A drunken driver had crashed his car through the front window and into the living room of the house next door. Since no one was hurt, the incident was an occasion for laughter and hilarity in the neighborhood; the driver looked particularly ridiculous sitting in his car in the middle of a wrecked parlor. But the next day, Terry picked out the nicest of the potted plants she had in her apartment and took it next door to the woman whose house had been wrecked the night before.

The neighbor fondly recalled that kind gesture two decades later at the time of Terry's death. No matter how troubled or sick she became, Terry did such things all her life. I could tell a thousand stories like this one that poured in from across the country after her death.

Returning to USD in the fall of 1975, Steve was invited by Terry and Bob to share a small farmhouse they had rented a few miles outside Vermillion. It was an unhappy experience for all three of them. Largely because of Terry's heavier drinking, which Bob constantly complained about, the two began to quarrel frequently—sometimes resorting to physical blows.

Warmly liked by both Bob and Terry, Steve served as a buffer and sometimes eased the conflict. That fall, Steve, who was also beginning to drink excessively, observed the first of Terry's blackouts and collapses from intoxication. "She seemed to be getting drunk more frequently," he says.

After two months of trying to moderate the increasingly angry battles between Terry and Bob, Steve moved out. The fighting became more intense, and a month later, as winter approached and life on the isolated farm became drearier, Bob and Terry moved back to Vermillion and occupied the bottom floor of a house. Her closest friends—Nikki, Steve, and Carol Brady—could not understand why she and Bob continued their battling relationship. Steve believed it was because Terry needed the quiet strength of Bob and admired his work as editor of the school paper. As for Bob, he liked Terry's personality and was proud of being the boyfriend of the daughter of South Dakota's senior senator and recent presidential nominee. He dreamed of one day working in Washington as a congressional aide—a goal he eventually achieved.

Terry became increasingly worried about her life: the drinking, the battles with Bob, and her academic difficulty. She confessed to Steve that she was finding it increasingly difficult to concentrate in her classes and to maintain regular attendance.

As for her friend Jeff Ferrill:

I traveled to South Dakota several times to see Terry. We continued to write and talk by phone, but I could tell by our conversations about Terry's "new friends," especially a guy named Bob, that she would not return to Charlottesville or to me.

We continued to see each other off and on whenever Terry was home for holidays or vacation, but while Terry and I still shared much, I felt she had grown more distant.

I think it was in the fall of 1975 that Terry told me that her drinking had become a real problem and that she was attending AA meetings. I think that by admitting to me that she had a drinking problem, she felt our friendship would end. Of course, she was wrong.

Terry and I talked by telephone numerous times and saw each other infrequently until I married in the spring of 1976. After that we corresponded several times a year. After my divorce in 1978, Terry visited me several times in Charlottesville or we saw each other in Washington.

In more recent years Terry would call me sporadically but never talked much about her problems. She wanted to know about my life and if I was happy. The last time I spoke with Terry was in the spring of 1993, when she was hospitalized at NIH. I think she really wanted to see me, for I learned recently that she called my mom and sister trying to locate me. When we talked, she said that she would be leaving NIH shortly and would call me when she moved into an apartment. We never talked again.

I will always remember Terry as a very special person in my life who always encouraged me when I was down, who taught me how to care about others and about myself. She was a person full of compassion, wit, and "true grit." She certainly gave more to life than she took from it.

I vividly remember Jeff's coming to see Terry at our Washington home on the day before he was married in the spring of 1976. He and Terry talked for several hours. Late that evening, when I went into the living room to say good night to them, I mentioned to Jeff that I understood his wedding was the next day. "Well," he said, looking fondly at Terry with a smile tinged by sadness, "that all depends. Terry could change that tonight if she would just say the word."

I was struck by the anomaly of a young man on the verge of marriage pleading with his old friend to come back to him. He loved Terry dearly, and she loved him.

Why then her rejection of Jeff in favor of Bob Martin? I believed then, as I do now, that Terry moved away from Jeff because she knew she was developing a drinking problem that would destroy any intimate and permanent relationship. He was too normal, too disciplined, too ambitious to live with someone like her, she likely thought. It wouldn't work. Their memories of shared joys would turn to conflict, bitterness, and disillusionment.

Jeff would have risked all this to regain Terry. How I wish that could have been.

Perhaps Terry's self-diagnosis was the realistic one. But as I read in her journals of her hunger in later years for "someone to love and protect me," I think of Jeff—now an investment banker, real estate developer, and loving husband and father. Terry, without alcoholism, could have been a superb partner. Perhaps even more to the point, if she had had someone like Jeff beside her during her disease, it might not have ended fatally.

Terry at our Washington home in 1989, with Marian (left) and Colleen (right).

F I V E

"I became Dad's special girl."

I have carried an image of myself that I am of average intelligence. I can't stand that perception of being average. It has been with me all my life and kept me from delving into any interesting work.

[Terry's journal, 1982]

My own view is that, as a person of considerably *above* average intelligence, imagination, and perception, Terry was distressed that a combination of depression and alcoholism prevented her from functioning at the level of her capabilities.

Her problem was not "average intelligence" but above-average vulnerability to alcohol and depression. With the passing of the years, that uncomfortable fact became increasingly clear not only to her but to everyone who knew her.

Terry was twenty-six when she graduated from the University of South Dakota on May 8, 1976. Although this was nine years after her graduation from high school, it was a major achievement, considering her handicaps, five years in Charlottesville for psychoanalysis, plus time out in 1971 and 1972 for the presidential campaign.

Upon graduation, Terry was uncertain about the road ahead.

She did not feel that her college education had equipped her for a job that was intellectually or professionally challenging. "I don't know of any career that I would want to go into without further schooling," she wrote, several years after receiving her B.S. degree.

Knowing of Terry's indecision about her future, her sister Susan invited her to move to Madison and live with her family. Sue and her husband, Jim Rowen, needed someone to care for their two boys, Matthew and Sam. Jim, the son of longtime *Washington Post* and *Newsweek* economics journalist Hobart Rowen, was administrative assistant to the mayor of Madison. Though he and Sue had grown up in Washington, D.C., they had met each other at the University of Wisconsin, where they became active in the anti–Vietnam War effort. They eventually gave more than a year of superb work to my presidential campaign—taking their infant son Matthew with them.

Arriving in Madison in the early summer of 1976, Terry fell in love with the city. Madison has interests and advantages that are unusual for a city of under 200,000. It is both the state capital of Wisconsin and the home of the splendid University of Wisconsin with its over thirty thousand students. It boasts excellent newspapers, a first-rate public school system, and two large lakes, Monona and Mendota, around which the city has developed. These two lakes offer scenic richness and a wide range of recreational activities in both summer and winter.

Terry moved into the modest home of Sue and Jim and helped with the care of their kids. Always an excellent and enthusiastic swimmer, she gladly took four-year-old Matthew swimming every day at nearby B. B. Clark beach on Lake Monona. One-year-old Sam was too young for such activities, but Matthew recalls those summer excursions with Terry (and frequent subsequent evenings when Terry was his baby-sitter) as one of the delights of his childhood.

Always able to identify easily with the interests and emotions of children, Terry enlivened their imaginations, sharpened their wits, asked them questions, and listened to their answers. She filled their minds with stories and poems and drew their attention constantly to the glories of nature.

Sue was concerned, however, about one problem: her sister's drinking had become more serious in recent years and was beginning to affect her emotional life. In late-night conversations, she was startled to hear Terry relating the hurts and wrongs she had suffered within our family—mistreatment by her sisters, insensitivity and neglect on the part of her parents, and the general dysfunctional character of the whole family. As she would relate these family wrongs, her face would fill with anguish and she would begin to weep.

Sue was unable to relate to these sorrows and angers because she had not perceived the kind of family ills Terry remembered. She believed that her parents were loving, and she did not regard the sibling rivalries of her childhood as that unusual. In addition, when she thought about the concerns and difficulties of "the family," to her that meant her own family—Jim and her children—not the family she had left behind to attend the University of Wisconsin twelve years before. She was amazed to discover that Terry, now twenty-seven, was still speaking as though she were a child.

Sue gradually concluded that Terry's emotional development had been arrested at the adolescent level because of the impact of alcohol and other drugs. She was still, in some respects, the young girl dependent upon parental support and yet sometimes resentful that she could not break free from it. At other times she was hurt and angry that her parents and others were not more supportive and understanding of her needs.

After countless hours of reading through Terry's journals and letters, I have belatedly learned much of what was going on in her troubled and searching mind. My own discoveries have been dramatically underscored by a perceptive book called to my attention by Eleanor, *Reviving Ophelia: Saving the Selves of Adolescent Girls*, by Dr. Mary Pipher. These words leaped off the pages of Dr. Pipher's book as I sought a more coherent understanding of my daughter's unresolved internal struggles from adolescence:

> Some girls are depressed because they have lost their warm, open relationship with their parents. They have loved and been loved by people they must now betray to fit into peer culture. Furthermore, they are discouraged by peers from expressing sadness at the loss of family relationships—even to say they are sad is to admit weakness and dependency.
>
> All girls express pain at this point in their development. If that pain is blamed on themselves, on their failures, it manifests itself as depression. If that pain is blamed on others—on parents, peers, or the culture—it shows up as anger. This anger is often mislabeled as "rebellion" or "delinquency." In fact, anger often masks a severe rejection of the self and an enormous sense of loss.

This seems to be what happened to Terry. As a little girl, she found her happiness and security within our family—especially with her parents. This relationship was fortified by her knowledge that she had a special champion in me. As she grew older and I became more politically involved, she lost some of the time and attention I had given her, but this loss was offset in part by the pride she felt in my growing prominence as a nationally known figure. In a sentiment frequently noted in her journal, she relates a conversational line: "I said, he is my father (feeling proud because he is a respected public figure)—my self-esteem has often been derived from this fact."

In her adolescent years, however, she was—like most teens—heavily influenced and shaped by her peers. It was the pressure of her friends and the society of the 1960s, as well as her own venturesome nature, that took her into a lifestyle at variance with her parents: abuse of alcohol and other drugs and an unwanted pregnancy that she was ill prepared to handle.

She blamed herself for what she saw as violations of her loyalty to her parents and their values. Not willing to reject her peers and their values, she felt separated from, if not abandoned by, her once treasured family.

She worried about exchanging her unwanted pregnancy for the emotional pain of an abortion and the consequent sense of loss. She condemned herself for the highly publicized marijuana arrest that might have ended her dad's political career. She told me that when I discovered her early sexual experience leading to abortion, followed by the drug arrest in South Dakota, she believed she was "no longer Dad's special daughter."

Just as Dr. Pipher has observed, these adolescent ventures into alcohol, pot, LSD, and sex led her into a deepening sense of guilt, failure, and separation from her earlier self and her standing in the family. She blamed herself for all of this. And just as Pipher concluded after looking closely at many such adolescents, Terry slid into a deep depression by the time she was in her late teens.

Then under the probing of psychological counselors, she came to attribute her troubles to a family who failed to understand her and male partners who failed to meet her needs for the love and attention she deserved. The result was a shift of her depression into a constantly recurring anger that she carried to her death.

She swung back and forth between depression combined with a deep love for her parents and siblings—and her two daughters—and anger toward those she perceived as having dealt her an unjust hand, including her parents, her siblings, and her several male partners.

In the search for the culprit that made her unhappy, depressed, fearful, or angry, or all of these, she, her counselors, and her family frequently failed in the early years to identify a major source of her mounting problems: she was an alcoholic. Terry was so articulate and convincing in explaining her difficulties that it was easy to overlook the role of chemical dependency.

There were doubtless many psychological and social factors contributing to her problems, but none of these could be seriously addressed as long as alcohol was the master demon controlling her life.

AFTER LIVING WITH Sue and her family during the summer of 1976, Terry rented a small apartment on nearby Spaight Street. She supported herself with a part-time job and occasional care of Sue's children. But as her drinking problems intensified, she for the first time put herself into treatment for alcoholism.

This brought her temporary sobriety, and she developed a relationship with a young man in Madison named Jon Rowe. When the relationship turned problematic after several months, she became emotionally ill, tormented by jealousy and regrets over the difficulties with Jon and with her life. She lay down one day on a Madison street until she was taken to the psychiatric ward at Madison General Hospital.

We asked her to come home to Washington, which she did. Jon accompanied her—finding a job and his own apartment. Terry was clearly suffering from an emotional disorder—essentially depression—that was so intense that at the urging of a medical specialist she underwent electric-shock therapy. Ignoring the warning of her doctor that electroshock was dangerous if combined with alcohol, she followed this dubious therapy with a quart of heavy liquor that nearly ended her life. Her vital signs virtually disappeared, but thanks to the alertness of her older sister Ann, she was rushed by ambulance to the emergency room of George Washington University Hospital. An experienced team of nurses and doctors immediately went to work on her, and she was revived—still in critical condition.

Frightened by this close call, I called Dr. Lawn Thompson, our longtime family doctor. "My God, George," he said, "I feel so sorry for that girl—and for you and Eleanor. But I can't think of anything you can do that hasn't already been tried. She's an awfully tough case. All we can do is hope that she can get into recovery and stay with it." The reaction of Dr. Thompson, a sophisticated, highly experienced doctor who would have done anything he could to assist our family, typifies the bafflement of those who want to be helpful in cases of alcoholism but don't know how.

After this near-death crisis, Terry enrolled for several months in an excellent rehabilitation halfway house for women in Arlington, Virginia. While living there she began working as a staff aide with the Senate Indian affairs subcommittee, headed by my South Dakota colleague, Jim Abourezk. She remained sober during this period. But, worried about a relapse, she returned to Wisconsin and enrolled in another halfway house in Chippewa Falls for several weeks.

Returning to Madison, she had the good fortune to become a friend of a recovering alcoholic named Peg, who lived with her husband on a farm a few miles outside the city. They were a wonderfully compassionate and helpful couple who were struck by the painful contrast between Terry's winsome personality and her frequently losing battle with alcohol. After careful thought, they invited Terry to live with them at their comfortable old farmhouse. Terry not only accepted—she fell in love with her newly supportive friends and their home.

Beginning on October 7, 1980, Terry experienced six months of sobriety with her friends. She then moved to an apartment in Madison and remained free of alcohol for eight years. This period of her life included a wide range of enjoyable friendships, public service employments, a lengthy romance, and the birth of her two daughters.

The decade of the 1980s was for the most part an enjoyable and productive chapter in Terry's life. Partly through regular attendance at AA meetings and partly through her always gregarious relationship with her neighbors, she cultivated many close friends. During my visits with her in Madison I always noticed that when she was not at work, she spent much of her time on the telephone, calling her friends and being called by them.

After my election defeat in the Reagan sweep of 1980, I asked Terry to join me on a lecture tour that took us to several Western states. She loved that rather relaxed tour of Colorado, Utah, California, and Montana. I was speaking primarily on university campuses—a lucrative and stimulating activity in my post-Senate years. But this tour was set up to allow some time for enjoying the scenic West.

In Utah, I persuaded my traveling companion to make her first attempt on skis at Snowbird Resort near Alta. A very inexperienced skier myself, I nonetheless set out to be Terry's instructor. After helping her to mount her skis, I was fastening my own skis when Terry involuntarily began to slide toward the beginner's slope. Yelling with a mixture of fear and excitement, she moved too quickly across the snow for me to catch her before she piled up in front of an advancing skier. He narrowly missed her, but a few minutes later, we saw two stretcher bearers picking up a badly injured skier on the adjacent ski run. We still had fun at the ski lodge, but the ineptitude of her instructor probably ended Terry's interest in learning to ski. I was not enhanced that day in her eyes as an athlete!

From the ridiculous to the sublime, we drove from Snowbird back into Salt Lake City and visited the Mormon Tabernacle with its majestic proportions and matchless acoustics. Visitors were allowed to press a button that started a recording of the tabernacle's famed choir. The recording that wondrously filled the great tabernacle was the old hymn "I Need Thee Every Hour." Terry and I were transported by the overpowering, beautiful harmony of one of the world's great choirs singing this lovely old song of the faith. As we stood there holding hands, I saw Terry's glistening eyes reflecting the spiritual inspiration we both experienced in this unique place of worship we were visiting for the first and only time. Recalling that day, I asked that this old familiar hymn be sung at Terry's funeral thirteen years later.

When we arrived in Helena, Montana, following the Utah stop, I reminded Terry that Helena had experienced a famous earthquake nearly a half century earlier, in the 1930s. Unbelievably, as we entered our hotel suite a few minutes later the building began to shake. We were experiencing a minor but definite quake. First the accident on the ski slopes of Utah a couple of days earlier, and now an earthquake. Terry playfully suggested that I had become too dangerous to be accepted as a travel guide. She had been sober for more than a year prior to this trip, and there were no slips on the tour. She responded warmly to my praise of her courage and discipline. It was a good time for Terry, and for me, that I still treasure.

There was one minor irritation on an otherwise enjoyable tour. Each time we occupied another hotel suite, Terry would tie up the phone line talking to her friends back in Madison or Washington. The long-distance charges aside, I was unaccustomed to waiting for the phone. When I expressed my annoyance, she retorted: "Dad, I've never complained about your calls. I have friends to call, too." I begrudgingly yielded the point. Years later, I read a report by one of her counselors of Terry's activities at the detox center shortly before her death: "She loved to talk about her travels with her dad." Which was what she was discussing in those calls she was so eager to complete so many years ago.

Leafing through her battered telephone book, one is struck not only by the evidence of an unusually large network of friends, but also by the closeness of the circle—as testified to by the well-worn pages. The little book also carries an undated recovery plan she had sketched out:

> *First year—not take first drink and continually make that first priority—*
> *Learn 24 hours a day to go through things without taking a drink—*
> *1. Go to AA mtg. every day—share—open my mouth and talk*
> *2. Writing out my story as a first step*
> *3. Be walking example of the Big Book [AA] no matter what others are doing*
> *You're a tough case—this disease has you by the throat—*
> *be extremely vigilant and disciplined with my time to stay close to my program.*
> *Decisions—*
> *Ask God to guide me and trust that he is. Sober buddies—within a year or so of my sobriety.*

Terry followed this plan faithfully, for the most part, in the 1980s; and as always, she devoted much time to trying to understand herself and to nurturing her inner self. I wonder if there was a day in her adult life when she failed to devote at least some moments to pondering the nature of her emotional concerns, conflicts, needs, and aspirations. I wonder if she ever let a day pass without thinking how she could become a better person. I wonder if she ever failed to be kind and responsive to someone she saw in need.

Terry, more than any other person I have ever known, was obsessed with knowing her own inner thoughts, fears, angers, loves, and anxieties, and with finding their meanings and origins. There were times, however, when she grew weary of this endless quest. "I've been rereading some of my earlier journal entries," she once wrote. "I hate to do this because although my thoughts were honest thoughts, they are the same crap over and over again."

Terry's emotional needs were probably greater than either her family, her lovers, or her friends could possibly meet.

I was sometimes uncomfortable talking with her because I would make some casual observation and she would respond with intensity, "Well, what do you mean by that?"

Doubtless, many of her inner problems and her inability to resolve them either stemmed from her chemical dependency or were aggravated by it. "Several years ago it became clear to me I had a drinking problem," an undated journal entry notes. "I had come to depend on alcohol for my confidence and self-esteem. I tried many times and many different ways to quit, but fell back repeatedly. It just seemed too difficult considering most of my friends drank; most social situations revolved around drinking. After years of struggle, I finally reached a point of acceptance that I could not drink and had to change my life in significant ways in order to assure that."

When Terry moved into her own apartment in Madison that fall, she went to work as a preschool teacher at the Red Caboose Day Care Center. The job was low-paying, but she enjoyed being with the children and quickly became a favorite with them and their parents.

She had a remarkable way of relating to children, talking to them and perceiving their wishes, needs, and hurts. She was one of those rare adults who never talk down to children; rather, she engaged them as equals. "When our children were with Terry, it added to their happiness and to ours," a Caboose Center father told me gratefully many years later. "Invariably, when I picked them up they would chatter excitedly about interesting and delightful experiences with Terry during their day at the Caboose."

She conscientiously structured daily activities for the children and held regular conferences with parents, supplying a written evaluation of each child's growth and of any problems she detected. By all counts she was an excellent caregiver for her young charges. She thoroughly enjoyed this job.

This child-care experience and her earlier days with Sue's children fostered a desire to have children of her own. She talked frequently to her sisters, her mother, her friends, and me about her longing to have a child. That desire was enhanced by the unhappy memory of her terminated teenage pregnancy.

Regrettably, our society places a very low economic value on the work of caring for children. Some of the best human beings in the community are frequently found at day-care centers or among elementary-school teachers. Their work is invaluable as they shape the minds and emotional development of society's most precious assets—the children who will become its future. Yet, the pay scales are shockingly low—barely at the minimum wage level.

Faced with a need for more income, Terry left her work at the Red Caboose after one year, although she continued to help out later as an unpaid volunteer. She found a job as a legislative assistant with two members of the Wisconsin state assembly and worked in their offices at the state capitol for the next year. Her responsibilities included researching legislative issues, responding to constituents' requests for information and other assistance, and monitoring committee hearings. This was a fairly happy year for Terry, and she made a number of new friends who enriched her life. But she had to give up the job when a series of medical appointments made it difficult to meet the demands of two busy legislators.

Long interested in the issues of mental health, Terry learned of a challenging job opening in this field under the sponsorship of Goodwill Industries in Madison. She was hired and then worked for the next four years as a counselor of mentally ill persons in a transitional residential care program. The work was difficult and sometimes hazardous. One mentally disturbed patient stabbed a coworker of Terry's to death. On the whole, however, Terry found her work there satisfying and stimulating, and the center performed an invaluable service for many troubled individuals. Her own personal struggles with depression and chemical addiction gave her insights and a sense of compassion. "There but for the grace of God go I" was a thought always in Terry's mind when she was with another person in trouble or hurting in any way.

During her years at Goodwill, Terry met an intelligent, energetic coworker named Ray Frey. Married and the father of two children, he was going through a divorce when he and Terry became acquainted.

When I went to Wisconsin in the fall of 1984 to campaign on behalf of presidential nominee Walter Mondale, Terry was on hand to welcome me at the Madison airport and to escort me to an open-air rally in front of the state capitol, where I addressed the crowd. I recall her shining face as she listened to her dad's account of the state of the nation. But she could scarcely wait for me to finish speaking before introducing me to her new friend Ray. We visited briefly before I had to move on to television, radio, and press interviews on behalf of Mondale's candidacy. Ray was a little intimidated, if not embarrassed, to be meeting me in the spotlight of a major campaign rally with the state capitol looming in the background.

I was aware, however, that Terry was anxious for me to offer some kind of initial reaction. This was obviously more than a casual friendship. She was falling in love. After continuing to work together and to see each other socially for several months, Ray and Terry began living together. The following year, Terry gave birth to her first daughter, whom she named Marian after Eleanor's deceased mother. At Terry's urging, Eleanor and I were in the delivery room with her. As an old-fashioned male whose previous experience with such events was pacing a hospital corridor, I found this eyewitness participation both thrilling and painful. Terry seemed to know that if her emotionally reserved dad actually observed the birth of her daughter, it would produce a special bonding between my first granddaughter and me. She was right. I felt as though I were part of the birthing process.

From the moment that little creature came surging into the world, she seemed to me to have made a decisive statement of intent that she was never to be ignored. She has had a special grip on me ever since—in considerable part because she has always reminded me of her mother.

I must confess that I so empathized with Terry's every motion during labor that when it was over I had severe stomach cramps, as though I had been in labor myself. I was also almost too weak to stand after all those labor pains!

Two years later, Terry and Ray had their second daughter, Colleen. She, like her older sister, was an endearing, somewhat feisty child. She also made clear that she was not to be ignored. These two little girls soon became as close to each other as any children I have ever known, and they continue to be so. Perhaps because of their mother's difficulties, Marian and Colleen have come to rely heavily on each other. They play together endlessly, and each seems to draw pleasure from the achievements and good times of the other.

Before Colleen's birth, I had been deeply concerned because

it did not seem to me that even after seven years of sobriety, Terry had the emotional strength to care for a new baby in addition to two-year-old Marian. Unfortunately, Terry overheard me expressing these concerns to Eleanor. She reacted tearfully, telling me that apparently I thought she had "screwed everything up again." Actually, she admitted some misgivings of her own, given her fragile emotional makeup and the fact that she and Ray were unmarried. Needless to say, we all fell in love with little Colleen after she came onto the scene. But Terry was overextended. She did not work outside the home after Colleen's birth. This was fortunate in that she could give full-time care to her children. But it also meant she was cut off from the structure and stimulus of professional work. Her days and nights, without domestic help or a nearby mother, were absorbed by the demands of an infant and a toddler.

Terry was also concerned about her relationship with Ray. He worked hard at his social services job, and on returning home in the evening he frequently helped out by preparing the evening meal or laundering the clothes. But perhaps because of fatigue and the strains and stress of the day, as well as his own reserved nature, he was not prepared to listen to Terry's accounts and concerns of the day. She resented that some of his private hours were taken up with legal and family matters with his ex-spouse and their two children. She was also hurt by what she regarded as his lack of emotional response.

Beyond this were the nagging questions about marriage. Why didn't Ray take the lead in asking her to marry him—the mother of his newly arrived children? If he should ask her to marry him, should she accept—considering her view of his lack of emotional warmth and support?

"Do I want to get married to Ray?" she asks in a journal entry of September 1985, four months after Marian's birth, while she was at home with us in Washington.

Can I wait another six months or a year to see how we do before I make that decision? The thought of living with Ray frightens me in a way. I need, as a new mother, a more total involvement from him—an emotional connectedness that I'm not sure he is capable of. What is the alternative? Fairly frightening as well. Single parenthood. Why do I want my family close to raise my family? Both my older sisters did it—came home to have their first babies. I think it speaks more to the immense change and responsibility of being a parent. Men don't seem to experience this at all the way women do. I think women sense they don't really have an equal partner in this with their spouses. It is women they want to be with. Women who love and care about them. I feel much more loneliness now than I did before with Ray.

Then she adds:

Depression is with me today. I'm so prone to it, and I believe it is largely from years of negative thinking. I seem to need to suffer and be sad— there is a grief in me that I must unleash and let go of. Calling Ray today and hearing his seeming indifference as to when I returned upset me. On the positive side, I think he was actually just relieved to know when I'd be home.

During most of the 1980s, Terry worked at improving her physical health and enriching her spiritual life. Living on a limited income, she insisted on a healthy diet for herself and her family. Her one physical impairment that she believed was a result of her earlier drinking was hypoglycemia—a chemical imbalance that required her to avoid sugar and carbohydrates. She conscientiously avoided not only alcohol, but any other items that might injure her health. Her diet depended heavily on vegetables, fruits, whole-grain cereals, fish, poultry, and low-fat dairy products. It was necessary for her to eat often, but in small portions. Paradoxically, when Terry was not drinking, no one was more conscientious about diet and other health factors. She extended the same care to her children. During her visits to our house, she gently chided me that as the longtime chairman of the Senate Select Committee on Nutrition and Human Needs, I was setting a bad example by consuming too much sugar, fat, and cholesterol. I thought that I was being cautious enough on these matters, but not according to Terry's standards. When under stress or fatigue she occasionally smoked a cigarette or drank too much coffee, she worried about the impact of these minor lapses on both her body and her spiritual health.

Gradually I'm getting free. Diet, meetings, meditation, and medication are all helpful tools. But also seeing more clearly that it just may be safe to take small steps to be more visible, happy, talkative. I don't need to hang on to this sadness that is family-rooted. My anxiety can be ended with faith. The good works that I do to be in God's will will bear fruit— I will know peace and happiness. Learning to love Ray these past few days has been exciting—fortunately he has been responsive. I know he won't always be but I'm benefitting from the immediate feedback now. I found out today I'll be working 30 hours weekly. I'm grateful I can contribute to the family budget more—it felt good to tell Ray. That is part of my commitment to our relationship. [May 15, 1986]

The following year, Terry and Ray came to our home for Christmas with Marian—Terry was pregnant with Colleen. Despite my concern over the pregnancy, it was a happy two weeks. I recall Terry's joy, as well as my own, over the close relationship that was developing between Marian and me. She was also pleased that Eleanor stood with her all the way relative to her second pregnancy. Eleanor and Terry chatted endlessly about the joys and concerns of nurturing little Marian and getting ready for Colleen's birth in March. Ray and Terry were also discussing their future lives in a positive, hopeful manner. Ray had established a workable understanding and settlement with his former wife and his two children, and Terry had completed over six years of sobriety. They happily told Eleanor and me that they were engaged and hoped soon to be married.

As an old-fashioned Methodist, I strongly favored this course. Some measure of ambivalence lingered on in the mind of each of them, however, and the marriage prospect seemed to dim in the months after they returned to Madison.

Writing in her journal about her love for Marian, Terry notes: "She doesn't tolerate the fighting between Ray and me. . . . A home of love is what she needs and deserves, and so do Ray and I. . . . This can be a home of joy, peace and love—a place of safety and serenity for all of us."

During her years of sobriety, Terry drew strength and enjoyment from her active involvement with the AA Twelve Step Program fellowship of Madison. She attended the meetings faithfully, several times a week and sometimes twice daily. Other participants were among her closest friends. She found pleasure and satisfaction not only in sharing her own concerns and victories with her companions but also in encouraging others to remain sober.

She never missed an opportunity to persuade friends with a drinking problem to get into recovery. I have been amazed at the volume of letters, phone calls, and personal conversations that have come to us since her death from people testifying that she helped to save their lives by pushing them into recovery. Her intuitive and perceptive talents and her own long struggles gave her a rare ability to convince other alcoholics that recovery was a vital and workable course.

Terry's close friends in Madison and Washington, both inside and outside AA circles, were too numerous to enumerate. Her need for camaraderie and affection and her warmth toward others seemed limitless.

But her struggle to sustain an ongoing affectionate and supportive relationship with Ray did not succeed. As always in matters of this kind, it is not easy to affix blame. But in the summer of 1988, Ray and Terry separated. A sad and tortured year followed Ray's departure. Terry struggled incessantly with her feelings of abandonment, anger, resentment, jealousy, and sadness, and made attempts at understanding and forgiveness.

I feel so sad at Ray's leaving. Like a lost child. [August 28, 1988]

Dreamed this morning about living in a big house with Ray. I'm still angry as I remember the abandonment. [August 29, 1988]

I'm feeling a lot of guilt for the breakdown of my marriage—like I drove Ray away. It hurts so much. . . . He was so distant—did I push him away? [September 13, 1988. Terry frequently referred to her years with Ray as their marriage and their separation as a divorce, although they were never formally married or divorced.]

Sleeping more difficult—waking sad, sometimes just wake up and find myself thinking of him—last night about making love, and how intimate that was . . . and now he doesn't talk to me, I don't look at him, I don't touch him. I do miss that. [September 29, 1988]

Ray controlled me in the marriage by being a martyr and making me thus feel guilty. By rarely expressing anger or any emotion about how I treated him, he made me suffer more guilt. My apologies were neverending. My rage was never-ending. [October 3, 1988]

Today a celebration for me—8th anniversary [of sobriety]. I'm glad I remembered. It is poignant, especially juxtaposed with the final ending of my love relationship with Ray. Gosh my heart saddens and heavies as I write those words. [October 7, 1988]

I woke up this morning missing Ray, feeling all the stuff and energy of memory—times making love, that we have some history together and now it is totally disconnected. [December 2, 1988]

[Her older sister] Ann's birthday today. I'm relieved I've got a nice gift on the way to her. . . . Last night went to Ray's and witnessed something very painful and angering for me. Sue and Ray were there. [Sue was the woman Ray established a relationship with after leaving Terry.] Sue had dinner laid out. Ray's apartment looked cozier. Painful for me to see how separate he has become. . . . I feel ashamed and very rejected that he chooses to get love from Sue and not me. . . . In truth I do not envy their relationship. . . . I know I don't want to go through another relationship like I had with Ray—looking to another for all my needs— trying to control them, to not feel the anxiety of my own separateness. [March 19, 1989]

God I long for easier, calmer days. This last year has been very difficult. I know I've got to really process the reality of my own childhood—it seems scary and yet unreal. Joan and Jill [her therapists] both say at least part of my anger now is about childhood, not just Ray's abandonment. My current obsession about Ray is extreme anger that he so lightly broke up our family permanently to get involved with Sue. . . . I still need to own my responsibility in this matter. [March 12, 1989]

Recovery from grieving results from setting recovery as an essential goal and from living each day as it comes, dealing with both the regular routine of living and our deepest emotions. We are recovering when we can look at life ahead as worth living. Full recovery involves the perspective to realize that someday we will look back and know that we have fully grieved and survived life's darkest hours. [April 15, 1989]

Marian's birthday was very painful for me. I didn't realize until after my session with Jill that I was fearing her birthday because of the feelings it would evoke. . . . I wanted so much to use and tried to get some pot. I still want some. I wonder if it would be destructive. [May 28, 1989]

Memorial Day depressing for me—starting about 12:30. I was obsessed with using. . . . I can in no way anticipate what would be sabotaged if

I used. . . . I think I'm in the final stages of grieving—depression and then acceptance. [May 30, 1989]

I smoked pot yesterday. Feeling physically lousy and spiritually as though it were a relapse. I don't want to smoke anymore. I feel its profound destructiveness in just one day of it. . . . My associations with pot are omnipotence and then shame, profound shame . . . because of its strong emotional connections with my past—high school—how lonely and guilty and ugly I felt in my family. [June 30, 1989]

Even in her 1980s decade of sobriety, Terry's addictive personality is always manifest—tormenting her mind, demanding that she be absorbed in herself, long for love and approval, want to be needed, blame her troubles on others—especially her parents, siblings, and lovers. I suspect that even her displays of compassion and concern for others resulted in part from her need to affirm that others had also run into trouble with life.

Looking back on her earlier years, she wrote in her journal on November 10, 1987: "I began caring for sickly animals and birds. I needed to feel important. I cared for the wounded animals. It was a way for me to feel my strength—to care for something helpless, dependent."

She became deeply engrossed with the "wounded child" syndrome—sometimes referred to as the "inner child." Encouraged in this direction by some of the psychological therapy of the moment, she began to imagine that every anxiety, every fear, every raging moment, and even her vulnerability to addition were the result of some childhood wrong committed against her by Eleanor and me, Ann and Susan, relatives and boyfriends. She once enrolled in a course for several weeks during the "wounded child" fad.

As I have learned more of Terry's life, I have come to a deepening conclusion that she was at her best when she was conscientiously involved with the AA Twelve Step Program—focusing on staying sober and recovering from alcoholism one day at a time. She was at her worst when, sometimes stimulated by psychologists, she looked backward in self-pity to the injured child suffering from the perceived misdeeds and ignorance of others. It is inevitable that all of us are affected in the present by our personal history. We may need to understand that history before we can fully cope with our current personal problems. But it is hazardous and, I believe, counterproductive to become frozen in time by an obsession with past wrongs and errors. At times, Terry seemed incapable of moving forward because of her preoccupations with her memories and perceptions of the past. And, of course, regardless of what psychological ills were revealed, such efforts were meaningless without sobriety.

A Woman's Journal, the name given by the publisher, was a companion journal whose pages she filled between April 1987 and January 12, 1991. At times overlaping the journal from which I have quoted extensively above, it tended to focus even more on her inner struggles and the abuses she perceived at the hands of others. One sees the stage for relapse being relentlessly set, first pot smoking and then alcohol.

> *Am feeling a heavy sadness inside. I know, or think, it is childhood pain. . . . I'm so damn angry that I didn't have a childhood, that so young I was already feeling alone. . . . It just seems that I remember too well whenever I was happy, joyful, visible, I got smashed down. . . . I'm deeply sorry that I hurt myself so much. No one meant to hurt me. And I didn't mean to hurt me. I want to be healed, Jesus. It's not right that I should want to die. Why should I die because my parents were too self-centered to take care of me? [September 3, 1987]*

> *Teresa, you have taken on the task of finding out who you are. . . . If my hurt child within shows herself and I smash her down with judg-*

ment, as I was smashed down in my family, I am not helping myself.
[September 1987]

Tonight was the first wounded child group. I didn't like it very much
and have some anxiety about sharing too soon who Dad is. I feel
ashamed that I was wanting so much to insure that I would be noticed
and taken seriously. [October 12, 1987]

This was a recurring problem for Terry. She was very proud
that her father was a prominent national figure. She frequently
drew on this fact to enhance her own sense of importance. At
the same time, she worried about this because it seemed to make
her acceptance by others dependent on me rather than on her
own worth as a person.

By beginning to gradually acknowledge my early painful experiences,
I will be able, perhaps for the first time, to find meaning for all those feel-
ings. Then I can begin to comfort myself, knowing that I was not re-
sponsible for what happened. . . . I think of the time at Lincoln School,
especially [1965–66, when she was sixteen]. I was depressed when I was
there—missed my parents terribly, and Bill. Suffered tremendous aban-
donment when he left me. My mom often tried to help me when I went to
her, but mostly I remember her wanting to change me, not being able to
meet me where I was. I grieved. I shouldn't have been sent away. I cut
my hair so I wouldn't look sexual to my father and be a reminder to him
that I was sexual and got pregnant. I felt like I lost my dad and was so
focused on that—and I'd lost a great deal more: my virginity, my baby,
my security, and then Bill. The only way I felt I could tolerate all those
losses was to totally enmesh myself in Bill, and my fear was unbearable
when he left me. I had no choice but to take drugs [a failing effort to re-
cover Bill by joining him in his drug sessions]. I had to be near him, be-
long somewhere. My parents thrust me again into a new setting [this
was the Quaker settlement house in Washington where she served one
summer as a volunteer assisting needy children] in the hope that I would
stabilize, find myself. And it would have been O.K. if the wounds had

been acknowledged and taken care of. It would have been a good plan if I already didn't feel so ashamed that I could not quite fit into a healthy environment. [November 1987]

Trying to apply the perceptions she had gained from her own childhood, she laid down some guidelines she wanted to follow as a parent with her own child, two-and-a-half-year-old Marian:

1. *I love Marian.*
2. *I inform her of upcoming changes.*
3. *I explain things in her world to her.*
4. *I point out interesting things for her to look at.*
5. *I take time in picking out books I think she will enjoy.*
6. *I am conscientious about her nutrition.*
7. *I am conscientious about her health care.*
8. *I am careful of how I talk to her to avoid shaming statements.*
9. *I am spending extra one-on-one time with her.*
10. *I sing to her, rub her back, and read her stories.*
11. *I take her to the zoo and to the park.*
12. *I tell her I'm sorry when I've blown it and left her feeling badly.*
13. *I've tried to make her room cozy and warm for her.*
14. *I often give her choices.*
15. *I don't rush her all the time, even if I want to.*
16. *When I remember, I often handle her body gently when bathing, changing.*
17. *I do reading and talk to people on how to be a better parent.*
18. *I'm seeking to address my wounded child issues.*
19. *I'm trying to sort out ways I can be more loving to her father, to model more intimacy than there has been.*
20. *I enjoy her!*

She is a wiser soul than I. She is strong and forgiving. Never, never have I hurt her out of any place except my own brokenness and woundedness. . . . I am ever caring and ever determined to parent her, and

Colleen, lovingly—and Teresa, this means parenting yourself lovingly first. I've been deeply shamed. I've internalized self-disgust, and if it takes me years, I will expose every area where I was made to feel shame and see it for what it was. I will not be tyrranized by myself. [November 1987]

A year later, she wrote of how she should be with Marian:

View her as a promise rather than a problem or a project. Enjoy her when she is around. Smile often. When she speaks, listen. When she proposes, consider: "Well, let's see. Would that be a good idea or not?" See her as the process of living and learning. When she fails, offer comfort rather than condemnation. "It doesn't matter. Now you know that doesn't work, so it won't have to happen again." Sometimes let her all but hang herself to discover something she needs to learn. [November 10, 1988]

By February 1988, she had begun occasional use of marijuana, which she referred to as a revival of "pot addiction."

Much of her journal is erratic and sketchy after this date. Then after Ray departs, there are signs of increasing inability to manage the two little girls by herself, leading to a serious alcoholic relapse in the summer of 1989.

I don't like being stoned around my children (marijuana). Marian sensed my distance and it frightened her. She kept crying, "I want my daddy in the same house. I want to go home." [July 29, 1989]

Still smoking pot. I still like it except when I'm around Marian and Colleen. I am basically disinterested in them when I'm high. [August 11, 1989]

The relapses that followed Ray's departure in mid-1988 ended eight years of sobriety, but Terry made a vigorous effort to stop drinking. At the Recovery House in Milwaukee, which she en-

tered in late October 1989, she worked successfully to achieve a
sobriety that lasted for over a year until Christmas 1990.

*I remember well how my disease treated me, how it abused me. And every
time I started to get well and happy, it looked even harder for a way to
hurt me again. I will think of a name for this disease that is a part of
me, but not me. [November 21, 1989]*

*Did I ever feel so intensely the need to get my father to love me, to come
home to us, to approve and be proud of me as I have Ray? If I could
only move from focusing on Ray to the arena where I suspect these feelings originated. Daddy—remember the little girl so much wanting to be
special. Jill tells me every little girl goes through a time where Daddy is
so important—to affirm sexuality, to approve of emerging sexuality.
Nothing any of us children did to get his attention, to get him to come
home and be a father, worked. In his ego-omnipotence, he thought he
could sweep back into the family and change things from the outside in—
he never got it that the trouble was in the hearts of his children. How
could he when he didn't know the source of his drive? He found a way
to effectively avoid his own internal wounded self through political ac-
claim—"narcissism," Jill calls it. A little girl, who I can hardly relate
to, and yet she is right here with me acting out the same need to change
Ray (Dad). Get Ray (Dad) to come home. Not to just come home but
be emotionally available and emotionally committed to love and nurture this family. [Fall 1989]*

*As I look at these precious, totally innocent pictures of my babies, I feel
so sad at the anger, impatience, and shame I put them through—Colleen
and Marian learning to eat and my fatigue weighing so heavy on me,
screaming at them for being messy. . . . I look at my babies and I just
know that we are going to be a strong family—the three of us. I imagine us in a nice home, a fireplace, yard, and a kitty. Dear Jesus, I pray
for a loving visit with my girls. [November 29, 1989]*

Write three things I need today:
1. Conversation
2. To be told I'm pretty

3. *To have my pain validated*
  My disease wants me dead.
      [December 13, 1989]

I haven't learned how to enjoy being chemically free. I still long for the
life when booze was my friend [undated, in 1990]

Terry with Eleanor at our fiftieth wedding anniversary, October 31, 1993.

S I X

"Three things I need today: conversation, to be told I'm pretty, to have my pain validated."

T ERRY'S LIFE AFTER the summer of 1988 was so chaotic—such a mixture of hope and despair, love and resentment, sobriety and relapses—that it is bewildering to piece the story together. It is difficult to tell a coherent story about an incoherent life. The story is further complicated by Terry's increasing confusion and her contradictory accounts of what was going on in her life as alcoholism befogged her brain and tortured her spirit.

Alcoholics and their advisers frequently speak of "hitting bottom"—meaning that the disease progresses to such depths that the victim can sink no lower and still survive. This stark reality sometimes leads the alcoholic into a desperate commitment to recovery. But it more likely leads to further disasters and an untimely death.

Terry seems to have hit bottom several times after 1988, but she did not give up the struggle for recovery. Nor did she succeed in achieving it in any real sense. What both amazes me and breaks my heart is the incredible grit, grace, and humor that she maintained in the closing years as she battled the stalking killer that would give her no peace and no mercy.

In the midst of my search for both the order of events and the content of these turbulent final years, I discovered a personal document written by Terry in 1992—a candid account of events and relapses in recent years. It may have been simply an effort to clear her own mind by sorting out the tangled pieces of her life. Or as I have suspected from many of her journal entries, it may also have been the work of a person with a sense of history who wanted to include some of the hidden aspects of her troubled life. It is not a pleasant story.

> *Summer '88—went to Arizona with Ray and our girls to visit Ray's family. Argued with Ray's mother—I left Ariz early with girls— drunk on plane—several times before Ray returned had to have Jim take care of Marian and Colleen. Got sober.*

> *Oct. '88—Ray left for good*

> *1988—Got job at [Wisconsin state treasurer] Charles Smith's office*

> *Mar. '89—Colleen's birthday—still sober*

> *May '89—Marian's 4th birthday—pool outside—still sober*

> *June '89—My 40th birthday—party with Joe, Susan, Ernie, Marian, and Colleen—took Ativan [a tranquilizer]—eventually I started smoking pot—drinking?—crying with Joe—he left scared.*

> *1989—Katy's—smoking pot—imipramine [an antidepressant], very scary, high anxiety. Would get Marian to Woodland school late, go stoned and hang out, not aware of tension it was causing.*

> *1989—on AFDC, food stamps, child support. Late summer—kicked Ray's apt. door in. He had me arrested and jailed. Mom came night of arrest. Went into treatment within a week or two in Milwaukee, Oct. 1989.*

For the last weeks in 1989 and most of 1990, she worked hard in the Milwaukee treatment program, which combined the AA recovery formula with psychological counseling. After five months, she rented a pleasant apartment in Milwaukee, got a clerical job, and continued an outpatient recovery program for the next nine months. During her inpatient care, she was given a pass on weekends to see her children in Madison. After she gave up the Madison duplex and acquired an apartment in Milwaukee, Ray would drive the children halfway to Milwaukee, and Terry would meet them with an old Chevrolet I had given her and drive them the rest of the way to her apartment for the weekend. It was not the most convenient arrangement, but the weekends were generally happy times—and Terry was sober from October 1989 until the end of 1990.

I did enjoy it and my children enjoyed it. I went to regular meetings, called my sponsor, but I did limit intimacy, social times.

December 1990—moved back to Madison—I drove to D.C. for Xmas with Marian and Colleen—very proud of myself as to how well I planned it. And that I conquered fear of driving that distance alone— never driven more than 5 hrs. alone. Also proud that I wasn't asking for money for plane tickets. Was very hurt when my sister called to apologize for talking behind my back with Susan about their resentment towards me for Dad helping me out financially.

I drank a few days later—the night before Christmas. No one ever knew because I stopped it right away. Drive back to Madison after Christmas holidays. Started drinking about two hours away from Madison—was pretty drunk when I got to town, snowing, drove off elevated driveway. Got drunker, screamed at Marian and Colleen out of my own fear about drinking, they were sitting on the couch, both crying. I told them Grandpa George would be coming in the morning and make everything O.K. I wanted them to feel safe. I felt very unsafe.

I did get job at Madison General Hospital, but too much stress—I had girls 4 evenings a week—get them to school and get to my job. . . . didn't like my sponsor, my landlord or other tenants or apartment—never really unpacked. . . . started drinking at work, quit with nothing else lined up. Drinking getting out of control. Did get sober for close to 2 months, but unhappy, seemed like things didn't get better. . . . Drunk for Colleen's 4th birthday party. Passed out halfway through, woke up on the bedroom floor. . . . I didn't want to cut back on my time with girls—didn't want to admit to Ray I couldn't handle it. [Ray had the girls on the weekends.]

Eventually, my drinking out of control and I had no more outside responsibility—no job, no children, no AA contact. Was staying drunk for days at a time, only leaving apartment to get more alcohol. [Ray assumed custody and care of the children.] Wouldn't know what day it was or how long I'd been blacked out or passed out. Nighttime would be a nightmare. So much fear. And no more alcohol. Couldn't pay rent anymore and couldn't get it together to find another living situation.

DWI and jail on way back from Milwaukee. Made attempts to get sober. Looked into halfway house—women and children center—not enough support to pull anything off.

Went to my friend Joan's—used her plenty but no other choice— lived there about a month started drinking her booze . . . another DWI while in liquor store parking lot. Ended up in St. Mary's for alcohol poisoning, kept leaving to get alcohol, decision made to put me in locked psych unit.

July '91—went to D.C., stayed sober until November.

Eleanor and I were alarmed and discouraged by Terry's repeated relapses—even after the prolonged and apparently excellent recovery program in Milwaukee. Partly in the hope that one more effort in the security of our Washington home might yet open the way to her recovery, we urged her to move in with us, which she did for the last half of 1991.

At our invitation, Marian and Colleen came to be with her for ten days in October. Terry began drinking several weeks after they left. She was so out of control that to protect her from self-destruction, we had her involuntarily committed to St. Elizabeths Hospital in Washington. Only the threat of intervention by a police team enabled us to get her into the hospital. After she was detoxed and stabilized there behind locked doors for two weeks, we brought her home. In a few days she was drinking again.

We then put her into treatment at Washington's Suburban Hospital, but she promptly broke out, went to a nearby restaurant, and collapsed from drinking.

Realizing that Marian and Colleen were coming to our home for Christmas, she made a supreme effort to stop drinking and did so for their arrival and for the next several days.

In past Christmases, we had arranged for Terry to have the guest bedroom at our home because of her two little children. This time, because our daughter Mary and her husband were coming home from UN service in Ecuador with their first baby, Caroline, we invited them to stay at our home and arranged a suite for Terry, Marian, and Colleen at the nearby Normandy Inn. This was a pleasant little hotel we had used frequently over the years. Eleanor and I had lived there for eight months in 1983 while our Connecticut Avenue condominium apartment was being rebuilt after a fire.

> *I was very angry that my parents told me I needed to leave the house and stay in a HOTEL with my children. Very jealous too of Mary— her new baby, the help she had, the money. And felt pain about what my children didn't get when babies. Felt ashamed to be dependent on parents' home at age 42, with no husband and children that no longer lived with me. Drank over it—turned to rage—threatened that if I had a gun I'd kill Mary, her baby, her husband, and my mother. Police called and took me to George Washington University Hospital Emergency Room. I woke up in 4 point restraints, where I lay all night. Next morning transported again to St. Elizabeths—allowed out for Christmas Day— started drinking immediately again at Sage's.*

Sage, a friend of Terry's, was a recovering alcoholic. She persuaded us that knowing all the tricks of alcoholics from her own experience with the disease, she could "stay on top" of any move by Terry to drink. She stopped with Terry at our home and picked up Marian and Colleen with the understanding that the four of them would spend a couple of hours together Christmas afternoon and then return the little girls to our home for the traditional Christmas dinner while Terry had dinner at Sage's home and stayed there indefinitely if she could remain sober.

Instead, when Sage took the girls and Terry to a family-style AA noon meeting in Georgetown to fortify the commitment to sobriety, Terry slipped out of the meeting to a nearby bar and filled up with vodka. Sage picked her up, brought Marian and Colleen back to our home, and returned the intoxicated Terry to St. Elizabeths—a sad twist for all of us on Christmas Day 1991.

Terry remained committed at St. Elizabeths until her girls had returned to Madison and Mary and her family had returned to Ecuador.

Reading *The Washington Post* early in January 1992 with Terry's committal to St. Elizabeths on my mind, I came across an item indicating that a branch of the National Institutes of Health that dealt with alcoholism and other addictions was willing to accept a few patients for a new experimental research program in alcoholism recovery. This news caught my attention for two reasons: I had the highest regard for the vast medical resources of NIH, with which I had become quite familiar during my long years in the U.S. Senate, and the program was free—an advantage that appealed to me after years of expenditures on Terry's earlier treatments and troubles.

The NIH effort combined the recovery principles of Alcoholics Anonymous with research into the impact of alcoholism on the physical organs of the body. It was an excellent program, which Terry found especially pleasant in part because she had a comfortable private room, good food, and a reading and television room—in sharp contrast to the spartan furnishings of St.

Elizabeths. In a sense, NIH was a haven for her, and she seemed to do well there during the six weeks of treatment and instruction. Eleanor and I also benefited from the family-related instruction on alcoholism as an addictive disease.

But as I have noted earlier, within the first hours following her completion of the program, Terry was intoxicated and passed out in a bar. I was never closer to total despair. Terry's report on all of this and beyond:

> *From St. Elizabeths transported to NIH Jan.–Feb.—drank day I left. March, committed to Georgetown University Psych Ward—Ashley—April–May—Relapsed in Madison—car taken away—evicted from apt.—got drunk—spent night with 3 white men and one black—made a point of telling them all who my dad was so they wouldn't think I was just a drunk and a loser.*
>
> *Terrible withdrawal began—vomiting, hallucinations, diarrhea, severe stomach pain. Began stealing all the time—all my money stolen. Charles verbally and sexually abusive. Police said he was dangerous. Called police on him—then I had no one. Ann [her oldest sister] came out, but I was in detox.*

When Ann telephoned to tell me that she felt Terry was on the edge of disaster—probably death unless we could find some method of "reaching her"—I called my friend and former Senate colleague Harold Hughes. Directing a recovery program especially for women in Iowa, Harold was himself a celebrated longtime recovering alcoholic. He had come to the conclusion that alcoholism hits women with special force and that recovery is more complicated and uncertain for women.

Generously, he opened the door of his program to Terry. I sent her an airline ticket to Des Moines and made arrangements with Harold to have her met at the airport.

Terry started drinking on the airplane en route and never gave the program a chance. She continued drinking even while supposedly in treatment. After telephoning her friend Nikki Abourezk in Vermillion, South Dakota, she went from Des Moines to live with this former college roommate.

While there, she served as a housekeeper for Nikki and cared for her children. Again the drinking started, and Nikki asked her to leave and assisted her admission to the Keystone Treatment Center at nearby Canton, South Dakota. When her drinking continued, she went to Sioux Falls, stopped briefly to see my sister Mildred at her home, and then, after spending a night at the detox center in Sioux Falls, checked into a motel for several days. She then called me and asked if I would arrange an airline ticket for her to fly from Sioux Falls back to Madison. I agreed to do so and called her cousin David Briles, who lived in Madison, to meet her at the airport. David called me later in the day to report with some alarm that Terry had not arrived as scheduled. Terry's journal tells why.

> *Don't remember where I was flying to, but was taken off the plane in Twin Cities, ambulanced to Hennepin County Detox—nightmare—went to Hazelden from there—started stealing, then drinking—then to detox center in Hastings, Minnesota. Scotty [another cousin] picked me up, got drunk at his home nearby, had to leave on bus to Madison, got drunk, couldn't stay at Sharon's. My wallet stolen that night. Tried to sleep outside at Ray's old apt. Neighbors called. Woke up in detox. Began series of staying with AA people.*
>
> *Ran out of places to go, no insurance, no halfway house, no money. Went to D.C.—stayed sober one month.*

While at our home in Washington that summer, Terry seemed to rebound quickly from the terrible previous weeks. Writing in her journal on August 29, 1992, she noted:

> *Five days of sobriety now. It feels so wonderful to pray again, to take care of my body, truly enjoying my family. . . . I went to my first Red-*

skins game tonight. I really enjoyed it. . . . After the game Dad played hymns on the piano and I sang as he played. I recognized it as the intimate moment it was. He has changed, and perhaps I have too. I don't feel so self-conscious around him. He knows where I've been so there's no use pretending I'm brilliant, ambitious, or very together. Just stay sober, unselfish, pray, and be grateful for the gifts of life I have been given and allowed to have despite alcoholism's best efforts to destroy them.

I recall this scene vividly. It was a warm, relaxed sharing of memories and music that stirred both of us. Terry had a soft, wistful smile that I can still see.

Then one night, she drove over to Washington's 14th Street in search of a marijuana dealer. Three men jumped her, took her money, and left her with a battered body. When they seized her billfold, she successfully pled with them to let her keep the pictures of her children. She recalls sitting in a bathtub later that night, hurting from head to toe and weeping. She began to drink again and lost control, and again we had to have her committed to St. Elizabeths.

She hated these commitments to St. Elizabeths, Washington's well-known hospital for the mentally impaired, but it offered the security of a locked ward for those bent on self-destruction. It kept her from hurting herself or others—and it kept her alive.

Terry then flew back to Madison at the invitation of a friend, Mitch Vesaas, to stay at his family home. Marian and Colleen came to see her once during this period. When Ray returned to pick up the girls, he found Terry in a drunken stupor.

About this time, one of Terry's friends told her of a new treatment center for female addicts that was just opening in a secluded area at the edge of Madison, named Venebue. I went to see it with Terry, and we were both impressed with its serenity and uncluttered space. Only seven or eight young women were there in treatment. Terry entered Venebue in late November 1992 and remained through most of December.

After a month, she wrote to Eleanor and me asking if when she was released in another month or two we would help her financially to resume a more normal life. "I do need to know if you will support me until I am able to be self-sufficient? I will need assistance for a place to live, utilities turned on and for moving my things from storage. I also need a bed and dresser which I intend to try and find secondhand. My hope is to find a house I can rent."

We agreed to all of this.

NOW, AS I write these repeated accounts of raised hopes and crushing disappointments, I wonder why Terry and Eleanor and I did not long ago say, "Enough is enough. This isn't going to work." But somehow, each time Terry got up her hopes and her strength, our hopes rose with hers and we tried again. In retrospect, we probably should have said: "We'll finance this thirty-, or sixty-, or ninety-day treatment program, but only on the condition that you go directly from treatment into a halfway house for at least a year. During that halfway experience you must get a part-time job for a few weeks and then a full-time job." That course was followed in the Milwaukee effort of 1990, but it should have been the standard for Terry. She was too confirmed an alcoholic to respond satisfactorily to one of the regular twenty-one- or twenty-eight-day treatment programs. In her case, as I suspect with many alcoholics, a month-long treatment is comparable to a beginning swimmer putting a toe in the water. I can't really explain satisfactorily to myself why we repeatedly went down that road to defeat. The Venebue program was no exception.

The problem with short-term sobriety for Terry was that she couldn't bear her life's pain without alcohol. Almost from the moment she moved into sobriety, she was beset by anguish—especially over the breakup of her family and the loss of her children. Sobriety brought pangs of guilt and regret over her failures, blown opportunities, and conduct painfully at variance with her moral standards. Sobriety was terrible for Terry. Her unusually perceptive and devoted friend Susan Robillard observed that for Terry "moments of lucidity created too much pain."

Having written so much of Terry's defeats and disappointments, I also see another Terry: the wit, the loving friend, the fascinating companion, the fighter who would never surrender, who kept coming back. Some years ago, I watched two ill-matched boxers in the ring—one with a reach four or five inches beyond his opponent's, plus a wicked one-two combination. The smaller fighter had only his pluck and his tenacity. He would take a hard left jab to the chin from the bigger man and before he could fully rebound from that he was on the receiving end of a jarring right-hand smash. I could not avoid attaching that image of the battered fighter to Terry. She would reel from the ravages of alcohol abuse, but when she became sober she was hit by the even more painful realities of sobriety.

Two of her many friends in Madison were Audrey and George Henger. Audrey wrote after Terry's death:

> I have wept over the loss of Terry—a gentle person who wanted me to believe in her—that's all. Sometimes I forgot and tried to help her. She would then disappear like a soft breeze, sometimes like mercury.
>
> She liked me to tell her the Ballad of Jack Armstrong: "I will lay me down to bleed for a while and I'll up and fight again." I believe she is now in a better place—a place of peace where she will no longer have to fight.

Another Madison resident who knew Terry even more intimately was her devoted therapist of many years, Jill Leventhal. After Terry's death, Jill wrote us:

I never knew anyone who tried as hard as Terry did to get well. She never gave up her faith, not even in her most desperate times. I know that her death did not signal her desire to die. She wanted to live, she wanted to stay sober, she wanted to have something in her life that was an anchor that she could hold on to. She just wasn't able to do it.

Two weeks before she died, Terry called me to ask if I could see her again. . . . This was so typical of Terry, to be once again trying to unravel the mystery that continued to lead her back to alcohol. . . . I had always found Terry to be a deeply spiritual person and I had hoped she could draw on this in her search for sobriety. . . . Terry never lied to me about her drinking; she was unwaveringly honest about all her shortcomings. . . .

She was very special, and I, like you, wished that I could save her. However, along with her tremendous desire to get well, she carried with her an overwhelming melancholy that had been with her for as long as she could remember; she was one of the saddest people I have ever met. She struggled with conflicting and intense feelings of sorrow, loss, rage, and emptiness. When she looked inward, she was faced with an abyss of loneliness, despite the qualities that others so loved about her. This was not because people did not care deeply for her, but because she could not feel their love when she was alone. . . . I have thought that you, too, knew that her struggles were deeper than even the intrepid battle she faced with alcoholism.

I believe that the key to Terry's life and death may be found around these central points: she was an alcoholic who longed desperately to be free of her alcoholism, but that disease combined with related emotional torment had so injured her mind and spirit that she was unable to live at peace without alcohol or some other drug. The one condition that was even more unbearable to Terry than intoxication was the emotional agony that seized her when she was sober. A supreme and relentless participation in all aspects of the AA program might have overcome this dilemma, but for whatever reason, Terry eventually lacked either the will or the strength required for such a commitment.

I believe that Terry was born with genes that made her vulnerable to drug addiction. I also believe that whatever the cause—marijuana, LSD, or alcohol, or her family and social environment, or her genes, or all of these—she was an emotionally distressed and depressed individual. What so baffled her friends and family was that her internal sadness and conflicts were usually hidden behind an endearing, delightful personality.

One longtime friend, Tierney, trying to describe her feelings about Terry, said to me: "I just can't tell you how good she was, how smart, how funny, how honest she was." That is a succinct portrait of Terry that has been expressed to me by countless friends over the years.

Terry proved that a troubled adolescent can also have a charming personality. We loved her and she loved us, but she could not love herself and wondered how *anyone* could love her. She seemed to be saying: *I can't accept my life and the way I have lived. I can't accept my tormented view of myself. How can anyone else accept me?* The best answer to all of this was to have a drink or two—or ten.

In her darkest hours she would sometimes say in effect and in various ways: *My father neglected me, my sisters resented me, my mother shamed me, the father of my children deserted me, I've lost my children, I have no home, I'm a drunk. How can I love any of this? How can anyone love this? It's time for a drink.*

Some people feel great when they are sober. I feel rotten. Let's have another drink. I was once a lovable little girl and people smashed me down. If they didn't love me then, how can they love the mess I've now become? I can't live with this. I need a drink right now.

Drinking may cause a problem, but it can't be as bad as the agony of sobriety. It may kill me to drink, and I don't want to die, but if I don't drink, life is unbearable. Let me have one more drink so that I can at least get out of hell for today.

Terry came to stay with us again on September 28, 1993. She did so at our urging, because, as Eleanor put it, "If she's going to die, I want her to be with us when she dies." Neither Eleanor nor I really expected Terry to die. I always saw her as a battler who would never surrender. But I shared Eleanor's feeling that Terry's relapse pattern was both frightening and life-threatening. Following her arrival, Terry wrote on September 30, "I want to be right where I am and not go anywhere—make myself safe."

A few days later she was drinking again. Begging me not to put her back into St. Elizabeths, she agreed to go to the highly regarded Seventh-Day Adventist hospital in Takoma Park, Maryland. She was there for several weeks. As almost always in these treatment centers, Terry "turned around" dramatically. Within a few days she became the darling of her ward. Each time I went to visit with her, she seemed so warm and cheerful that I would again conclude that this was it. Terry was going to be okay this time. I'd get my wonderful daughter back into my life. She was going to be sober and happy again. This time things would be different. Terry was going to get well.

On October 30, 1993, Eleanor and I were to observe our fiftieth wedding anniversary at Washington's Embassy Row Hotel with a party sponsored by our children. Terry desperately wanted to be in attendance, and the entire family wanted her to be there. I talked to her doctor at Takoma Park Hospital, Dr. Fred Risser, a longtime family friend, and he agreed to release her for a few hours with the understanding that someone be designated as her chaperon and make sure she got back to the hospital by midnight.

I think this was one of the happiest nights of Terry's life. She loved that party—the celebration of her parents, the toasts recalling our fifty years together, the photo sessions with the family. She glowed and joked and reveled from beginning to end. I recall so many of her happy expressions, embraces, warm exchanges, laughs, and tears of that magical night. One of her closest longtime friends, Dawn Newsome, was her designated chaperon, and she delivered Terry to the hospital at the stroke of midnight. She reported later that if there is such an experience as pure joy, Terry found it for that long, happy night.

One poignant moment remains in my mind. When Terry came into the beautifully decorated hotel reception area, wearing a new dress purchased by Dawn, I saw her pause at the door, look tentatively around the room, and then, with a brave smile, walk toward Eleanor and me. I was simply overwhelmed with a feeling of tenderness. My precious, fragile, terribly sick daughter, on leave from the hospital, dressed in the prettiest gown she could find, was desperately wanting to show her love for her mother and dad. I treasure a camera shot of her holding my hand and looking around the room for the rest of the family—a mixture of anticipation, anxiety, and pleasure on her face. I'd seen that look countless times during Terry's life.

She made it a point to talk to nearly every person in the room that evening, and dozens of them later told me of the joy that shone in her eyes and echoed in her conversation.

Two weeks later, she was writing:

I need to write this as tears well up in my eyes. Because truthfully I had no memory of what it feels like to quit drinking once I've started. Now I will list how it feels after 3 drinks to have to stop.

1. *Depression*
2. *Anxiety*
3. *Some fear*
4. *Agitation*

My body and mind do not feel relaxed, even though a nonalcoholic's mind and body would be relaxed after 3 drinks. My body is telling my mind, just one more really strong one would do it—coat the nerves and they'd stay coated and numbed. With all my being I would like to have been like the man who could drink a shot of whiskey every morning— like a cup of coffee—and leave it be. But what happens is that shot gives me a feeling of wholeness, and when it starts to go away there is artificial emptiness just as there was artificial wholeness. . . . I could weep and weep that the lie is still alive. How could I want to keep company with the same agent that has snatched from my grasp all that I have loved. God forgive me. Teresa forgive Teresa. [November 13, 1993]

Back at Takoma Park Hospital a few days later, she writes:

I had a positive experience here before, and I will again. Billie, Jane, Jasmine, Fred Risser, and Judie. Tomorrow the depression will have lifted and I will sleep well tonight. Tell Fred about difficulty reading, concentrating, and finishing projects. I'm much more comfortable with him. . . . sobriety is my only goal now. Tomorrow I'll get to see the place in Rockville [a rehabilitation and recovery center recommended by Dr. Risser] and I'll stay here until I can get in. [November 17, 1993]

Recovery from alcoholism represents a period of remarkable change. It's a bit like a second adolescence. The recovering person's body is something of a biochemical volcano, erupting from time to time in strange ways, shaping and influencing responses to ordinary events. [December 2, 1993]

Alcoholism—that was the hidden monster—alcoholism, the unconscious disease.

I feel peaceful again—most peace since I've been here. . . . Nothing ends life—death not linear. Calling Madison my hometown [at the AA meeting] and then saying, "When there's a blackout I was no safer than at 2 years old, out alone—and people did hurt me." [December 5, 1993]

The treatment at Takoma Park followed by additional care at Rockville seemed to be helpful for Terry, and she, Eleanor, and

T E R R Y

I went to National Airport to greet Marian and Colleen on December 18. Christmas was a week away, and it was a happy, festive time. But Terry took time to note in her journal: "When the disease reaches the stage where it severely impairs an individual's ability to control consumption, then 'moral' choices as to when to drink, or to cut down or control consumption, will become meaningless."

After enjoying two weeks with Marian and Colleen at our home over Christmas, Terry remained with us through January and February 1994. These months, however, were marked by more relapses and brief recoveries. Late at night, January 30, 1994, after a day of drinking, she called me into her bedroom and begged me to get her another drink. I refused. She then asked if she could borrow my car to visit a bar. I explained to her that it was after midnight and the bars were closed. I also pointed out that an ice storm that day had left the hill on which we live coated with ice. There is a drop-off at the bottom of the hill, and I feared that even a sober person, let alone one as intoxicated as Terry, would very likely encounter a disaster in trying to drive a car down that icy hill.

A half hour later I thought I heard a noise in front of our house. It was Terry, sitting in the driver's seat of a new car I had just purchased for Eleanor with the windshield wipers swishing futilely over the ice-covered windshield.

I went out to remove Terry from the car. She clung to the steering wheel, determined to drive down the hill. I could not reason with her and I could not dislodge her from the car. Her desperate determination frightened me. I'm a physically strong person; I was sixty pounds heavier than Terry; she was drunk and I was sober; yet I could not get her out of the car. It was a dramatic demonstration to me of the overwhelming power of an alcoholic's craving for alcohol. She was not concerned with the danger of a crash that might have claimed her life or someone else's. She was totally dedicated to one objective: more liquor for her tormented body.

Only the fear of a disastrous crash finally gave me the strength to pry her hands from the steering wheel and drag her from the car. I did not know that Terry had released the brake and moved the gearshift from park into drive. As she cleared the car, it lurched forward down the hill without a driver. Hitting the bare ice, it spun to the side and smashed with some force into the side of a neighboring house.

Terry had warned me forcefully an hour earlier that she could not go through the night without more liquor. I thought I was right in ignoring this warning. I was wrong.

The point of this story, however, is the incredible power of alcoholism to seize the victim's whole being. "Dad, my whole body is screaming in agony for alcohol. Please, please, please!" And then in a moment of forced gentleness, still pleading: "Dad, why don't you sit on the edge of the bed and just quietly have a drink with me." Possibly I should have done that on that particular icebound night at an hour when Terry was crying out for mercy from the depths of her soul.

Achieving a period of sobriety again for a few weeks after this incident, Terry asked if I would return to Madison with her and help her get settled in an apartment. She wanted me to commit ten days to this trip. I agreed to go back with her, but after finding a comfortable apartment for her on Farley Street and moving her furniture there from storage, I returned to Washington after three or four days. Needless to say, I wish now that I had canceled my appointments in Washington and stayed with her longer in a more relaxed fashion.

We of course did a number of things, as did Terry, for which I am grateful. All the treatment programs, detox periods, and hospitalizations were costly and also discouraging when they were followed by relapses. But those were times that gave her body and mind an opportunity to heal. Without those breaks in her drinking pattern, she would doubtless have died many years ago. Adding up all the time devoted to these periodic treatment sessions means that in addition to the eight years of sobriety in the 1980s, Terry had additional years of cumulative sobriety when her vital organs were healing from the damage of alcoholism. I'm glad that we tried repeatedly to open the door to sobriety for her and that she repeatedly got at least partway down the path of recovery.

I rejoice too when I recall the trips, the movies, the restaurant meals, the kidding, the fun, and the thousand quips we had together, a continuing reservoir of good memories.

But there weren't many quips or laughs in 1994. Within a few weeks after Terry and I had found the Farley Street apartment in early March, she resumed drinking again. Her medical and police records on file at the Tellurian Detox Center and the Madison Police Department tell that story in all its pathos and deepening tragedy.

MADISON POLICE DEPARTMENT:
April 14, 1994—Time 1:12 p.m.—[Terry living at 513 Farley]
Subject was found passed out sitting up against a fence. She was very intoxicated, she had a hard time keeping her balance. Her speech was slurred, she smelled very strong of intoxicants. She informed me that if she was taken home she would go back to a liquor store and buy some more alcohol. Said she had been drinking vanilla extract.
—Sgt. Bruce Beckman

TELLURIAN DETOX CENTER:
April 14, 1994—Time 1312—Client brought to detox by Shorewood Police Department and was placed on Protective Custody.

April 15, 1994—10 a.m.—Discharged from detox

April 16, 1994—10:07 a.m.—Admitted to detox.

McGovern was on a city bus very disoriented. Fire Rescue responded and determined there was no health problem or risk. McGovern was intoxicated. She had difficulty answering questions and could not stand by herself. We conveyed her to detox for treatment. She was incapacitated by alcohol.

On April 16–18 detox, Terry said she had been sober for 6 months prior to the April 14 detox. Said she was to start job April 18 and to see her children that weekend.

April 18, 1994—1:25 p.m.—Discharged

May 6, 1994—3:25 p.m.—Admitted to detox.

Transported intoxicated from St. Mary's Hospital. Passed out walking home from liquor store and taken to St. Mary's. "I hurt all over."

Talked of her coming family vacation at Outer Banks.

Prognosis for sobriety poor based on frequent admits to detox: 4-14-94, 4-16, 4-24, and 5-6.

Discharged May 8, 2 p.m.

May 17, 1994—3:30 p.m.—Admitted detox

Passed out on Capitol Lawn. Taken to University of Wisconsin Hospital and then to detox.

Discharged 5-23, 9 a.m.

July 5, 1994—1:25 a.m.

Arrested with man for disorderly conduct while intox. Found sitting with Joseph Skully behind closed shopping mall and restaurant. Admitted to detox.

Says first time she drank since family vacation at Outer Bank [June 17–July 1].

Discharged July 5 at 1:25 p.m.

July 16, 1994—Admitted detox
  Discharged July 19, 6:45 p.m.

July 25, 1994—Admitted detox 1:45 a.m.
  Taken to St. Mary's emergency room 8, then to detox.
  Discharged July 26 at 10:55 a.m.

July 27, 1994—Admitted detox 9:50 p.m.
  Discharged Aug. 1, 1994, at 9:55 a.m.

Aug. 4, 1994—Admitted detox 1:45 a.m.
  Arrested for taking 6-pack of beer—intoxicated
  Discharged 8-8 at 10:20 a.m.

Aug. 15, 1994—Admitted to detox
  Found passed out in storage room of Party Port Liquor Store

Regrettably, Eleanor and I were at the University of Innsbruck in Austria, where I was lecturing from July 1 until August 10. We were not in telephone contact with Terry during this period. But upon our return to Washington, I spoke with Terry's counselor at Tellurian, Gerry Kluever. She advised me that Terry was not doing well and might have to be committed. I confirmed my desire that she be involuntarily placed in long-term care if she continued to relapse. It is not a simple matter to have a person committed to hospital care against the patient's wishes. The Tellurian staff was slowed by the need to prepare a legal case demonstrating that Terry was a threat to herself. They also later told me that their personal affection for Terry made it difficult for them to take legal action against her when she was pleading with them not to do so. The staff was probably in error in postponing this action, considering Terry's record of continued, chronic relapse.

I'm going to let the records of the Tellurian Center and the Madison Police Department tell the story of Terry's painful progression toward death.

Aug. 17, 1994—Discharged 1:50 p.m.

Aug. 19, 1994—Admitted detox 3:17 a.m.
Terry found passed out in restaurant with head injury. Taken to U. Wis. Hosp. And then to detox.
Back of head-scalp injury

Aug. 19, 1994—3:17 a.m.
Brought—by police. Passed out. Head injury from unknown cause. Unable to walk—very garbled speech. *Danger to Self.* U.W. Hosp. Requested transport due to head injury and alcohol incapacitation.
Depressed. Passed out in a restaurant with head injury. Blood alcohol level .44
Discharged Aug. 23, 1994, at 9:37 a.m. 70 mg. Librium given in her first day of admission (Aug. 19—none needed after that)
Terry had Antabuse with her—apparently released to go with Art Lahey.
8-20   Pain neck from head wound in back of scalp. Could take several days for blood to reabsorb.
8-21   Terry wants to get back on Antabuse. Started to cry when she told counselor about the terrible cravings she has to drink.
8-22   Terry plans to live with Art Lahey at Horicon, Wis. Old friends—nothing sexual.

Aug. 29, 1994—Brought by police from emergency room at St. Mary's Hospital to detox with blood alcohol level of .36
Danger to Self
Taken to St. Mary's for CAT scan after friends thought she fell in her hotel room.
Terry drank at Art Lahey's after going there Aug. 23 from detox

Aug. 31, 1994—She cried when told she was drunk in front of Art's daughter
Art took her to Motel 6.

TERRY

Sept. 1, 1995—Discharged from detox 1:37 p.m.

Noted at 10 A.M. on this date that Terry shows minimal motivation toward sobriety evidenced by her discharge plan for herself and refusal of voluntary stay to assist a long-term recovery. Terry was told she could return to detox voluntarily if she realizes she may drink and wants to return sober.

September 2, 1995—7:37 a.m.

Teresa somehow ended up in Madison General Hospital Emergency Room. She was so loaded with alcohol she couldn't do anything without help. Placed in police car and taken to detox.

Passed out in lobby of a hotel and transported to hospital for eval.

Blood alcohol level .432

Hit head in falling at Holiday Inn.

Danger to Self

September 29, 1994

Gerry Kluever, her counselor, says Terry remains sober. Had enjoyable weekend with her children. Stress in her living situation.

Will start job this week on trial basis. Terry was told if unable to cope she could return to detox voluntarily. Terry expressed concern that she might be "biting off more than I can chew."

Told she needs to stay within her own comfort zone.

Terry says she may go to S.D. this week for presentation her father may receive (S.D. Hall of Fame).

Terry still in Horicon

Said she is seeing her daughters regularly and enjoying this. Has some anxiety however, as they will spend weekend with her and she has always had to drink to deal with this.

October 10, 1994—

Arrives per friend at detox, unable to walk

1: Strong odor of alcohol

2. Mumbling, slurred speech
3. Inability to walk
4. Disoriented—place and time
5. Reddened eyes, unable to focus
6. Unable to care for self
—Mary Greene, R.N.

October 11, 1994—
Resting in room.
Afraid because she is homeless and has resumed drinking—concerned where she will live—"Maybe I can stay at some AA friends."
"If they don't commit me, I want to go to Hope Haven [halfway house]."
Teresa expresses extreme remorse and depression over repeated relapses.
—Deb Day, R.N.

She was released to Hope Haven Halfway House on October 24, 1995.

MADISON POLICE DEPT.
Nov. 13, 1994, Time 2359
Hodge reported a female/white passed out at the bar. On arrival I contacted McGovern, who was passed out. . . . I was unable to rouse McGovern. Police officer Papp and I escorted McGovern out. McGovern was very unsteady on her feet. . . . I placed McGovern in police car and conveyed her to detox.
—Police officer B.A.
Bar personnel advised that she walked into the bar, ordered a drink, and then passed out. McGovern told me that she was taking Prozac.
Inappropriately dressed for cold weather.

TELLURIAN DETOX CENTER
Nov. 14, 1994—Time 0245—Admitted

A 45-year-old white female was brought to detox via Madison Police Department—being reported as missing from Hope Haven. Client was passed out at Red Shed bar—unable to walk—slurred speech—told R.N. at detox entrance unit she had started to drink in front of daughters.

—D. Day, R.N.

Client has tremors and receives Librium 25 mg.

—M. Greene, R.N.

November 15, 1994—

This writer shared her opinion with client that she has become a drunk who passes out in bars and becomes incontinent of urine. In this writer's opinion, client needs to put on hold her "spiritual life" through books and deal with the basic issue that she is an alcoholic. Client also shared that when she spent time with her daughter on Saturday she had wine with lunch and told her it was grape juice. This writer responded that children know more than we think they do and chances are daughter knew she was drinking. It is in this writer's opinion that client needs to work on self and spend as little time with children as possible for now. . . . Client is also unable to make safe choices in the community as she is presently homeless. . . . Client is unable to remain safe from alcohol when in an unstructured environment. Client will be reevaluated on Nov. 17, 1994, for possible discharge.

MADISON POLICE DEPARTMENT
Nov. 17, 1994—Time 1435

Officer Greg Martin and I were dispatched to 20th Century Books, 108 King St., reference a woman passed out and unresponsive. Upon arrival with Fire Rescue unit we contacted Teresa J. McGovern. The complainant, James H. Luttrell, stated that he found McGovern seated in a chair in his office.

McGovern was asleep and Luttrell could not wake her up so he called Fire Rescue. I noticed that McGovern's breath smelled heavily of alcohol, her speech was slurred, and she did not stand without assistance and had to be helped down the stairs. When I told McGovern she was going to detox, she tried to break away. She begged us not to return her to detox.

—Police Officer Chris Smith

TELLURIAN DETOX CENTER

Nov. 18, 1994—Time 0900

Client appears depressed.

Client has tremors, states, "I'm going to my parents' home in D.C."

Nov. 19, 1994—Time 1535

Client medically stable for discharge. Left unit per self.

Nov. 20, 1994—

Friend [Art Lahey] that client was staying with brought client into detox. . . . Friend stated that client had been drinking for two days. . . . Client opens her eyes, very somnolent, moans, needs assistance of two aides, nauseated. Client incapable of meeting basic needs.

Nov. 22, 1994—Time 1630

Client is discharged to stay at home of AA member [Kate Morgan]. Client pleased, stating that she and female friend would attend a play at her daughter's school. Client asked that message be relayed to friend Art if he stopped by detox. Art is to bring client's turtle to Williamson St. Cooperative where client will meet him at 6:30 p.m.

MADISON POLICE DEPARTMENT

Nov. 23, 1994—Time 2030

Madison Fire Dept. responded to Wong's Restaurant to check on McGovern. McGovern had ordered dinner and had apparently been drinking heavily. Upon my responding I contacted paramedic Scott Hermansen from Rescue #4. Hermansen stated that McGovern has a lengthy history of this behavior. McGovern was attempting to sleep in the booth she was sitting at when I arrived. Hermansen checked over McGovern and requested she be taken to detox. I then transported McGovern to detox.

—Police Officer L. Wing

TELLURIAN DETOX CENTER
Nov. 25, 1994

Client talked about a person named Kate [Morgan] who client says has 7 years of sobriety and has agreed to be client's sponsor. Client also says she plans to move into own apartment next week. Client was crying during most of the session. As client thinks about effects of alcohol on her life she fears that recovery may not be achieved.

Nov. 26, 1994

Client discussed hopes and fears of having a new apartment to move into near her children, of having a new sponsor, and another chance to develop a sober lifestyle. Client expressed fear of having another failure at attempting sobriety. States: "I don't think I could stand it again, another failure."

Client's frequent admissions to detox presents a questionable ability to care for herself and her basic needs in the community at this time.

Nov. 28, 1994

Client talked at length about her decision to try therapy with counselor she had experience with (outpatient in Monona) [Jill Leventhal]. Client states she was always looking for "something different" but realizes there's nothing she hasn't "tried" before. Client appears more open than in the past to look at changes needed within her rather than externally. She expressed awareness of fears that impeded her in attaining sobriety, and described support available to her (including Community Intervention Team and AA people helping her during upcoming relocation to new apartment).

Nov. 29, 1994

Review of Client's aftercare plan. Besides CIT [Community Intervention Team] and AA support and outpatient therapy, client will be living temporarily with female recovering friend and sponsor [Kate Morgan] and moving into new apartment in 3 days.

Nov. 29, 1994—Time 0957

Client left per self.

MADISON POLICE DEPARTMENT
Dec. 1, 1994—Time 1610

Police Officer Baker and I were dispatched to the above address, University of Wisconsin Hospital Emergency Room ref: a transport to detox. Upon arrival we contacted the Emergency Room staff who informed us that McGovern was very intoxicated and had a high blood alcohol level. McGovern who was obviously incapacitated by alcohol was placed under Protective Custody. McGovern was transported to detox where she was admitted.

—Police Officer Jim Strassman

TELLURIAN DETOX CENTER
Dec. 1, 1994—Time 2042

Client taken to U.W. Hospital via Madison Police Dept. after being reported passed out on a city bus. BAL=.420

A danger to self. Bloodshot eyes.

—Annette Larson, R.N.

Dec. 2, 1994—Time 0945

Client keeps asking to get out so she can try and regain her apartment. Client further reports that she stole beer from the workman at the apartment while the floor was being done. . . .

TERRY

This writer recommends that client be maintained on unit on Protective Custody because client presents a questionable ability to care for basic needs and safety.

—Rodney D. Simms

Dec. 2, 1994—Time 1330

Client requests use of phone on social side to call her landlord to get information regarding her down payment on apartment. Client is unable to use phone on Medical side as another client is screaming. Client is appropriate in request. After using phone on social side client waited by door to administrative side of building. Client proceeded to leave detox as housekeeper entered door. Client ran out administrative door. Client has no shoes, no coat, and no money: Madison Police Dept. notified of incident and that client remains on Protective Custody in detox.

MADISON POLICE DEPARTMENT
Dec. 2, 1994—Time 2001

Officer Fields and I responded to Meritor Park Hospital Emergency Rm for a Police Car Conveyance. McGovern had a blood alcohol level of .442. Emergency Room staff stated McGovern had been involved in some kind of disturbance involving another female on Gorham St. where she was ultimately conveyed by Fire Rescue to Meritor Park Hospital due to extreme intoxication. . . . We conveyed McGovern to detox.

—Roger B. Babor

TELLURIAN DETOX CENTER
Dec. 2, 1994—Time 2035

Client admitted to detox
BAL .440
Unable to care for self.
Needed assistance walking.
I believe this person is incapacitated

Dec. 3, 1994—Time 1410

Client states she called a cab and went to the downtown area. While downtown client states she went to the bank and got $, then purchased some footwear. After this client states she was concerned about an apt. she is currently trying to rent; so she went to the location. After visiting the apt. in the Williamson St. neighborhood she went to the liquor store, bought alcohol, became intoxicated. Client states to writer that she does not regret what she did due to her concern over not getting to an appointment to talk with landlord. Is sorry about how she went about it. . . . I recommend that this client be maintained at detox unit on Protective Custody due to the need to further monitor and evaluate client after excessive intake of alcohol. Client currently requires medical supervision due to past incidents of major withdrawal symptoms including tremors and diaphoresis. Client has been to unit many times in the past and does not maintain adherence to recommendations or advice given in past. Client currently suffers from active alcohol dependency.

—Terry Fox

Dec. 4, 1994—Time 1315

Client wanted to know if she would be allowed to go to a therapy session on Wed. Dec. 7 at 1330 located at the Verona Family Practice Clinic to see therapist Jill Leventhal. Client states the session was recommended by Gerry Kluever, client's primary counselor on unit. . . . I recommend that client be maintained at detox unit on Protective Custody due to her excessive consumption of alcohol. Client is currently actively alcohol dependent.

—Terry Fox

Dec. 5, 1994—Time 0740

This person's denial as to the seriousness and consequences of her alcohol use is intense. She appears to believe that she is in complete control and is making logical choices. I recommend that this client be treated confrontationally with facts of behaviors and consequences. Informed client that she will be maintained on Protective Custody due to her chronic habitual use of alcohol evidencing an inability to care for her health, safety, and basic needs. Multiple repeated detox admissions.

Dec. 6, 1994—Time 1000

Client reports multiple concerns re: housing, relationships, etc. Client was directed as to plans to prevent further life damage working with a sponsor to:

1. Hook up with psychotherapist to work with father of her children on reasonable visiting plan.

2. Look into group of women with children who are affected by alcoholism. (Deal with guilt, relationship, etc.)

3. Contacting women in neighborhood to be supportive of each other.

4. As soon as possible service work with Riverview club near new pending apartment. Progression of client's alcoholism discussed. Client admits if present plans fail feels long-term treatment is appropriate. States would not do in Madison but would seek long-term care with father's support.

Guilt over inability to deal with children when sober. Made appointment and plans for ride to therapist [Jill Leventhal] tomorrow.

Has sponsor and is working with her. Unable to care for self as evidenced by repeated admits, unpredictable behavior, deteriorating health.

—Gerry Kluever, Counselor

Dec. 7, 1994—Time 0800

Reviewed and signed discharge plan. States has problem getting appt. landlord—Reconsidered and will probably be ready this weekend—plus limited time with children. . . . Also has decided to go along with ex-mate relative to limited visits with children as "I don't have the energy I need to care for them." Reported ambivalence about support system she has set

up for self. If this doesn't work, I will go to long-term treatment. Discharge with Community Intervention Team to appt.
with therapist.

—Gerry Kluever, Counselor

Dec. 7, 1994—Time 0850

Client medically stable. Discharged from unit with Community Intervention Team member.

MADISON POLICE DEPARTMENT
Dec. 7, 1994—Time 2030

Officer Armagost and I responded with Fire Rescue ref. A
woman by the Williamson St. Co-op, 1202 Williamson St.
The woman McGovern was found in the co-op with towels
around her feet as she had been walking in the snow and cold
with only tennis shoes and wet socks. She had an odor of intoxicants on her breath, slurred speech, and could not stand
without assistance. She could not speak coherently and mum-
bled about a sponsor. McGovern was unable to care for herself and was incapacitated by alcohol and placed under
protective custody. She was conveyed to detox after being
seen by Fire Rescue.

—Police Officer Jerry Fouzel

Dec. 8, 1994—Time 1600

Terry's recollection the next day to the Tellurian staff of
events of Dec. 7 was as follows:

Reports ride to Community Intervention Team with CIT
member. Called father to co-sign for lease. Went to bank—
took out $550—"got nervous because I had so much cash" and
returned to CIT to ask that they hold it so would not be
stolen. Client did have Antabuse though chose not to use it.
Client states "from my memory" they kept the money for
me—"but I guess that did not happen." Client reports obtained wine. Went to St. Vincent's, bought scarf and socks
—they had no mittens. Had lunch with Marian at her
school/glass of wine. Went to apt. to give $ to landlord but

wasn't there. "I had hoped I had slipped the money under the door but called landlord to learn I had not." Went to Crystal Corner Bar—the last bar Steve [her recently deceased male friend] was in. Went back to apt. But locks had been changed—went to neighbors to get pen and write name and address for mailbox and taped to mailbox because expecting a letter—"as far as I remember, I only drank wine. . . . I remember falling and getting wet and being embarrassed hoping no one had seen me. . . . I went to the co-op to wash my face. . . . I don't remember anything after that until woke up here. . . ." Client informed commitment being pursued. . . . Client appears sad . . . depressed . . . denies suicide leanings . . . refuses to sign Release of Information for counselor to contact parents. . . . Client reports knew commitment was coming and asked father today to check into treatment program for her. Client reassured when asked if would have to "just stay here" that every effort would be made to get treatment for her. Client told will be maintained under Protective Custody until medically stable and able to care for basic needs due to alcohol dependence.

—Gerry Kluever

Dec 9, 1994—Time 0840

Brief discussion of client's pending legal commitment, client reports being aware of it via her primary counselor [Gerry Kluever]. Client claims she would still like to arrange treatment on her own but expressed belief that it's pretty much out of her hands now. Client's attorney is Yolanda Lehner who is "hard to reach." Overall, client appears resigned to being committed to alcohol and other drug abuse treatment based on her statements and dejected manner. She described the theft of her $600 as "the last straw."

Dec. 10, 1994—Time 0800

Reports she has been experiencing mild panic-attack. States she is upset about having all her money stolen, but states that most of the anxiety she is feeling is related to a pending involuntary commitment. States she has called her father and they will be making calls to see where she can get long-term treatment that her medical assistance will cover. States, "I don't want to get stuck in this place for a long time that won't even count."

Dec. 11, 1994—Time 1145

States she wants to have her primary counselor know that she set up an appointment with her landlord for 0900 on Monday 12-12-94. States she is looking forward to keeping her doctor appointment for a medical evaluation to see if having taken Prozac is preventing her from maintaining sobriety. Client expresses anxiety reference to commitment process. Wants to know if she didn't drink now if there was any possibility she could avoid the commitment.

Dec. 12, 1994—Time 0800

Client appears confused this a.m., denies having any trouble with memory and states "I'm just depressed." Client was confused as to whether or not medicines had been given.

Dec. 12, 1994—Time 0900

Client and counselor discussed plan for discharge this A.M. Request discharge to take care of things: see landlord, pick up social security check to replace money "borrowed" from deposit, close bank account and library card due to stolen ID, and to check with police for purse. Client informed plan is to pursue commitment with papers to be filed Wednesday and schedule her court appearance Friday. Client very concerned about where will be served, i.e. in public or with children, etc. Client encouraged to return here after errands. Client states will not return today. States will stay with sponsor "Kate" tonight and if she needs someone to talk to today will go to Community Intervention Team. Client also makes point—does not want sponsor, family, or friend Art involved in commitment proceedings. Client denies suicidal thoughts—states she knows what to do if feels like drinking will call or stop at Community Intervention Team, call detox unit, or call therapist or sponsor.

—Gerry Kluever

Dec. 12, 1994—Time 0900
  Client remains medically stable and is discharged to community per self.

—M. Greene

There are no more Tellurian Detox Center records for Terry—only a report from the Madison Police Department the next day that her frozen body had been taken to the St. Mary's Hospital morgue.

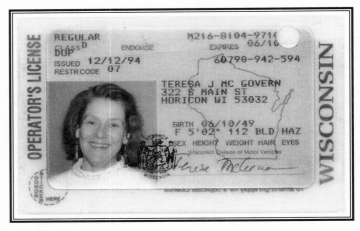

Terry's driver's license. The photo was taken on the last day of her life, December 12, 1994.

SEVEN

"My disease wants me dead."

There is no Angel of Death. When you die, an angel greets you to let you know you are still alive. And when an angel reminds us, for even an instant, of our own journey Home, our place of Origin, our highest Self, it has caused a miracle within us.

So wrote Terry in her journal a few weeks before she died.

Terry thirsted for spirituality—for the meaning and enduring values of life. She was always searching for a dependable "journey Home." She wanted to know her "place of Origin." She longed to reach her "highest Self." And unfailingly she sought to help others on their journey—especially if they were hurting.

When asked by an alcohol treatment therapist to identify "Ten Good Things About Me," she listed twelve:

    1. *I have a very caring heart.*
    2. *When not drinking, I am a creative and loving mother.*
    3. *I have a good sense of humor.*
    4. *No matter how many times I have fallen into relapse, I keep striving to get sober.*
    5. *I'm willing to help people in pain.*

6. *I love a lot of different people.*

7. *I go out of my way to not step on ants.*

8. *I believe that the political and social causes I've worked for have been very humane.*

9. *I'm devoted to my family.*

10. *All the volunteer work and professional work I've done has been in service to others: elderly, mentally ill, children, handicapped children, hospice work.*

11. *I long for spiritual growth and have been consciously drawn to it for many years.*

12. *I am intuitive and perceptive.*

These thoughts were found among her papers at the Tellurian Detox Center, where she spent her last days. They were accompanied by a second written assignment: "Why Do I Deserve to Be Happy?" Terry's answer:

1. *Because I am a caring person and want others to be happy.*

2. *I have two beautiful children who love me.*

3. *God has kept me alive so far.*

4. *Everyone deserves to be happy—it is God's wish for us.*

5. *Though not exactly healthy, I come from a family of good people who are all trying to grow spiritually.*

6. *I am intelligent and capable of creative and meaningful work.*

As Terry, always a sensitive and perceptive person, neared the end of her journey, she became even more so. Her answers to the assignments above were accompanied by a brief synopsis of her alcohol affliction.

My alcoholism is a chronic attempt to fill emptiness—to take the place of what alcohol has taken from me. . . . I need to set out on a journey trying to find out what is satisfying to me.

What did I do for the 7 years of sobriety that sustained me? In the middle of this alcohol-induced depression, it is hard for me to think of anything that would really be satisfying.

I do know that I value being a mother—that I would like to work again—have friends.

In still another therapy assignment, Terry was asked to list "Ten Issues Most Crucial to Me—What Is Wrong with the World?" Her answers:

1. *Lack of concern for the environment*
2. *Starvation*
3. *Sexism*
4. *Too much conformity*
5. *Maldistribution of wealth*
6. *Breakdown of family*
7. *Spiritual hunger*
8. *Too difficult to do what you really want to do (lack of options)*
9. *Self-centeredness/greed*
10. *Abuse of children, old people, animals*

When asked to "Identify Achievements at Different Points in Your Life That You Might Like to Write About," she noted the following:

1. *Getting sober*
2. *Finished college*
3. *Learned to swim*
4. *Public speaking—1972 Campaign*
5. *Summer of service at District of Columbia Settlement House on C Street*
6. *Learn/practice meditation*
7. *Trained two parakeets to talk*

To an instruction calling for her to define "My Ideal Life," she wrote:

A balance of education, work, and leisure. Keep a balance—don't get fixed in the past while working on it—be in the present, future-oriented— be aware of the good of today.

These personal documents summarize Terry's final struggle to assert her spiritual values against the demands of her addiction. These are the culmination of a quest that embraced much of her life as she struggled to nourish body and soul against the ravages of alcoholism and what she referred to as "alcohol-induced depression."

Of the hundreds of pages in her journals and letters, the responses above represent Terry's clearest awareness of her struggle. These simply expressed insights combine a humility, honesty, and perception that have added to my deepening admiration for my daughter.

She saw the vicious circle that alcohol had thrown around her. It first crowded out the other joys of her life; the resulting "emptiness" then demanded more alcohol to offset the lonely void. Others had told her that her depression and related emotional difficulties had caused her alcoholism, but she came to believe that it was the other way around: alcoholism was the cause of her continuing and deepening depression—"this alcohol-induced depression." Perhaps Terry would have suffered from depression even if she had not been an alcoholic. Certainly there are many depressed people who have had no history of alcoholism or other addictions. But one fact is certain. Alcohol is not an effective antidote for depression. Alcohol can be a brief exhilarating stimulant, but when consumed excessively over time, it is a depressant. Drinking to medicate one's troubles is a certain route to even worse troubles and worse feelings about those troubles.

"THE GOOD THAT I would, I do not," said St. Paul. "The evil which I would not, that I do. . . . The will is present with me; but how to perform that which is good I find not." I don't recall ever passing on to Terry this confession of St. Paul's that captured my imagination many years ago, but if I had, she would have said wistfully, "That's me, Dad."

That's the way it is with good people who become addicted. Their ideals and aspirations, their spiritual hunger, remain, but the addiction is in command of their behavior much of the time. Alcohol masterfully manipulates the war between ideals and actions.

I believe that Terry sometimes saw her experimentation with alcohol and other drugs as revelation—a path into mysteries of the self, the spiritual self.

Carl Jung, the great pioneering Swiss psychiatrist, advised the founders of Alcoholics Anonymous to seek spiritual healing of addiction. In his phrase *spiritus contra spiritum,* he was expressing his conviction that the craving of the alcoholic is partly a spiritual hunger that could be redirected and healed only by a stronger spiritual force. This is what AA adherents mean by "a Higher Power" capable of rescuing the alcoholic from an addictive force he or she is powerless to contain.

Alcoholics do not abuse drugs because they want to become addicted or even necessarily to become high for the moment. They hope to find in chemicals a way to feel better—just to be normal like other people. They may also "take a trip" on drugs to discover new insights about living and about themselves. Sometimes this works in the short run—as some artists, writers, and musicians have testified. Alcohol can relax the nerves, set free the imagination, loosen the tongue, warm the heart, and add to the camaraderie, romance, and warmth of human relations—if used moderately. But the alcoholic has no capacity for moderation or any other consideration beyond consumption. Alcoholism demands powerlessness of its victims. It insists on the final word in decision-making and judgment. Its claim is total.

At hundreds of meetings of Alcoholics Anonymous, Terry would take her turn with the prescribed AA greeting: "Hello. I'm Terry, and I'm an alcoholic." But in her private journal she wrote: "I'm not an alcoholic; I'm a human being with the disease of alcoholism." She had no doubt that she was an alcoholic, but she knew that she was much more than that—as do other alcoholics. Longtime participants in AA know, of course, that "denial" is the great curse of those trying to recover. That is why they insist on the repeated declaration "I'm an alcoholic." At some level, denial was a recurring problem for Terry.

She knew well the pangs and powers of alcoholism, but she also experienced the profound stirrings of the spirit within and around her. She readily accepted Dr. Jung's conclusion relative to his emotionally troubled patients: "I never encountered a patient whose problem was not at bottom spiritual."

During a time of sobriety in early 1994, Terry and I were having dinner in Madison at a restaurant near an apartment we had just rented. Listening to her views that evening I was struck again by the essential decency, honesty, and infectious wit of this ever struggling daughter.

"Terry," I said, "when you are sober there isn't a more lovable creature on this earth."

With a slightly sad smile she responded, "Thank you, Dad, but don't you think I might be a little bit lovable even when I'm not sober?"

Terry knew that she was never more than one drink away from intoxication, a blackout, or a physical collapse. There was never any moderate ground on which to stand. She was either in total sobriety or she was "smashed." And when she was smashed she was not always lovable—even to her little daughters.

She keenly understood all of this. She related with deep regret the times when she saw fear in the eyes of Marian and Colleen as they watched from the backseat while their inebriated mother tried to drive them around Madison. She constantly asked their forgiveness for yielding to alcohol or losing her temper with them.

"Please Describe a Blackout or Memory Loss You've Had," one of her treatment assignments instructed. She wrote:

I drove my daughter Colleen (then 4) and myself to Lodi for an interview as a live-in assistant to an elderly wheelchaired man. His son offered me a drink, which I took. My last memory was of Colleen sucking on an orange popsicle and she and I playing in the lake. I woke up in the middle of the night and she and I were in bed together naked on the second floor of this house. I quietly dressed her and myself, snuck downstairs, got in my car, and drove home. The only memory of the drive home is drinking the rest of a half pint of vodka and looking in the rearview mirror at Colleen in the car seat. I thought I saw fear in her eyes—and I felt ashamed. . . .

Shortly before this incident, while Terry was at our home in Washington with Marian, then age five, she started to drink while Eleanor and I were attending a social function. When we returned, Terry was inebriated, having vomited on a new beige carpet in our living room. Marian was taking care of her as though she were the mother ministering to a wounded child. There remains in my mind the image of this deeply concerned little girl with an arm around her mother, who was seated unsteadily halfway down the stairway. Marian was patting Terry's cheek gently with her other hand, pleading, "Come on, Mommy, I'll help you down to the kitchen and get you some warm milk. It will make your tummy feel better."

Incidents such as this deepened Terry's sense of shame, her loss of self-esteem, and her anguish—all of which called for still more liquor to ease the pain. She was beset with the pains of low self-worth for much of her life. I have been unable to discover a source of this seemingly self-inflicted misery, except for her alcoholism. All who knew her testify to her love for other people—and indeed for all living creatures, plants, and works of nature. She could love her neighbor, the sunset, or a homeless animal, but she could not love herself.

At times, she would write in her journal: "Be kind to yourself, Teresa. Be gentle with Teresa. Don't berate and abuse yourself, Teresa."

These admonitions would sometimes be accompanied by times of meditation, quietude, and careful attention to her mental and physical health. But more often than not she would fall into a sense of shame over the condition of her life. She doubted her worth and dignity as a person.

I believe that her declining sense of self-esteem and her craving for alcohol were handmaidens that fed on each other and repeatedly pulled her from sobriety into the merciful oblivion of intoxication. Reflecting on Terry's life and death, her youngest sister, Mary, wrote:

She has been spoken of as a cheerful person full of jokes and laughter. She was also known to be aggressive and biting. I believe the two behaviors were motivated by the same shame: the profound fear that she was not good enough, that she had to prove something—prove she was . . . what? Entitled to be here? I think that shame is the cause of more human folly and tragedy than is adequately credited. I think it is behind that obsessive need to acquire money and power, and the grotesque need to feel superior to someone. People of shame suffer so much. Their guilt and their anguish and anger can build a pain so blinding that they ultimately flee to the soothing relief of drugs and alcohol. We must learn to treat ourselves with greater kindness, less contempt and self-derision. That is why as a lesson of Terry's death I deeply believe we must work to criticize ourselves less, to feel less guilt, to stop the self-blaming.

No matter how many times Terry went down the treacherous road of relapse, she never ceased to search for a way back, a path to recovery, a sense of direction in her life.

On June 10, 1995—Terry's first birthday following her death—our family and friends spoke extemporaneously when we dedicated a memorial enclave to her at the Tellurian Detox Center, which was her home so often in her final years. My daughter Susan's tribute is worth repeating here:

> One of the responsibilities that has fallen to me since Teresa's death is to go through her things in storage and distribute them to the appropriate persons. On the one hand, this has been very painful, as the sense of loss deepens with each box that I open; on the other, it has been wonderful in that I have come to know her better than I ever did in life. I have been slowly reading her journals. I read recently that the purpose for our having been given life is for us to train our souls, and to improve our spiritual selves, and Teresa's journals show that she strove for this always. She was "done in" by her physical body—by those awful cravings for alcohol—but she had a beautiful spirit. I think the way she died was horrible, but I have seen that she did work to train her soul and to improve her spirit life during her struggle with alcoholism. If there is an afterlife of some kind, she entered that realm with a soul prepared. Essentially what is meant by "spiritual growth" is that we are to become more compassionate to others. Terry had that compassion . . . so I am grateful for her life and for her generous spirit, which lingers with us.

In modern times, people educated in the scientific worldview hesitate to talk about spiritual experience. We feel it is hard to

G e o r g e M c G o v e r n

express in a way that can be truly taken in by another. If we anticipate that others will not understand or, worse, will label us as ignorant for thinking our mundane experience touches the transcendent, we just won't talk about it. Terry did talk and write at length about her spiritual quest, sometimes in following the AA Twelve Step Program, sometimes because of her own impulses unrelated to any organized agenda. She wanted to be as trusting of a Higher Power as she would have desired to be in a close, loving relationship with a life partner.

She sought spiritual growth—not perfection—one day at a time. She understood that by confronting in writing or conversation her own weakness and darkness, she might find healing for her troubled spirit.

Susan has noted:

> Teresa's journal records her spiritual journey. Much of it describes a dark history of complaint, self-pity, and anger. She wrote mostly to vent and work through problems, to confront her darkness. Still, she was progressing spiritually all the while. Her journal fixed the movement of her daily experience in time, in words on a page, while her lived experience may have been transformed into something else immediately after the words were written. Those who practice the Twelve Step Program find that confronting weakness and failures of character opens the way to receiving strength and healing from beyond, from a power "higher than ourselves." The spiritual movement that may have occurred after Terry faced her own rage and pity was mostly implied, rarely written down, partly because of the evanescent nature of spiritual awareness. It is lived rather than written.

To understand the long involvement of Terry with the AA recovery agenda, it is necessary to be aware of the Twelve Steps, which all AA participants are asked to follow:

STEP ONE: We admitted we were powerless over alcohol—that our lives had become unmanageable.

STEP TWO: Came to believe that a Power greater than ourselves could restore us to sanity.

STEP THREE: Made a decision to turn our lives over to the care of God as we understood Him.

STEP FOUR: Made a searching and fearless moral inventory of ourselves.

STEP FIVE: Admitted to God, to ourselves, and to another human being the exact nature of our wrongs.

STEP SIX: Were entirely ready to have God remove all these defects of character.

STEP SEVEN: Humbly asked Him to remove our shortcomings.

STEP EIGHT: Made a list of all persons we had harmed, and became willing to make amends to them all.

STEP NINE: Made direct amends to such people wherever possible, except when to do so would injure them or others.

STEP TEN: Continued to take personal inventory and when we were wrong promptly admitted it.

STEP ELEVEN: Sought through prayer and meditation to improve our conscious contact with God as we understood Him, praying only for knowledge of His will for us and the power to carry that out.

STEP TWELVE: Having had a spiritual awakening as the result of these steps, we tried to carry this message to alcoholics, and to practice these principles in all our affairs.

Honesty and openness are the first requirements of the Twelve Step Program. Active alcoholics who have long suppressed the truth, hidden it from themselves, and lied to themselves and others about problems must open their eyes to the darkness and confess to others. Terry was honest, and, despite her tendency to look outward for the source of her problems, she eventually accepted responsibility for her part in generating her problems. "I am the problem, and I am the solution," she wrote during a late treatment program. This was a sign of spiritual growth, because, as C. S. Lewis's novel *Till We Have Faces* puts it, it is not until we know our own face that we can turn it toward the light.

A defect, a personal problem, can be thought of as an open wound. The wound may fester, or it may represent an opening to healing. Some healing comes with recovery and spiritual progress, but with alcoholism there is never a final cure.

The authors of the *AA Big Book* state: "We are not cured of alcoholism. What we have is a daily reprieve contingent on the maintenance of our spiritual condition."

For Teresa, healing came only with death, but in the meantime she had been in frequent communion with a higher power for many years. "She had her eyes and arms lifted up," said Michael Florek, the director of Tellurian. Terry spent as much time directed toward maturational and spiritual growth as she did in the grip of her self-defeating, hate-arousing, death-dealing disease.

Her disease did arouse a circle of hatred: self-hatred, which fueled conflict with others, which in turn brought more unkindness to her. She was a charismatic person whose warmth and humor won over people instantaneously. Some friendships endured throughout her entire life, but many others faltered from disillusionment, hurt, and chronic disappointment. Consequently, forgiveness became a chronic issue for her and for those in relationships with her, especially close family. Not surprisingly, the need to mend relationships through amends and forgiveness is a central concern of the Twelve Step Program.

As early as 1982, when Terry was thirty-three, she wrote in her journal:

> *I have to make the decision to stop wanting to be spiritual just to meet my own needs—to be honest enough to come clean so that God's grace*

*could enter my life and give me some direction and purpose. Prayer can
be used to establish an openness with God and others in order to love and
be loved.*

*I must admit that I need God, trust the promise of forgiveness, and
desire to be open to the spirit within me. I need to believe that there is hope
for me. Become aware of my need for God.*

Terry's spiritual quest began long before sobriety brought her
into the spiritual discipline of the Twelve Step Program.

Sue recalls some of the spiritual influences in Terry's growing-
up years in our family:

Her grandfather, Joseph McGovern, had been a fundamen-
talist Wesleyan Methodist minister. As an adult, she cherished her childhood experiences in Sunday school and
summer Bible school at the First Methodist Church in
Mitchell, not far from her home on West Fourth Street. At
home her father played his favorite George Beverly Shea
recordings over and over; during family drives in the car,
gospel or church songs rang out on the radio, while her father
told stories about her grandfather's life as a Wesleyan
Methodist minister. He had built churches all over the state
of South Dakota, after leaving an earlier life as a professional
baseball player. Her father told how as a minister's son he had
chafed under a regime of compulsory all-day church attendance on Sundays, unendurably hot and emotion-wrought
summer revival meetings that went on for days, and the strict
prohibitions against sports on Sunday, movies, dancing, sex,
alcohol, cigarettes, and swearing. Her father's chief early re-
bellion was to sneak into movie matinees every Saturday, and
he still considers these forays into the forbidden world as one
of the delights of his childhood in Mitchell.

In spite of the complaint about his repressive upbringing,
Teresa knew that religious wisdom strongly informed the man
that her father was and is. Were not biblical quotations sprin-

kled throughout every political speech he gave? Wasn't the
Christian Social Gospel an inspiration for his populist and sometimes radical political views? Teresa and her siblings were taught
Christian values directly, and they found childhood comfort in
the atmosphere of religious music. Teresa loved her childhood
image of Jesus ("Jesus loves me, this I know,/For the Bible tells
me so"). We would both weep with remembered joy, remembered safety, when we sang the old familiar hymns together in
the Methodist services we began attending again as adults.

Terry wrote in her diary of her spiritual journey:

*As long as I don't give importance to the realm of the spirit, I will feel
isolated and insignificant—and be compelled to seek constant people contact, sexual intimacy, eating, smoking, to feel better. When the ego is
cut off from experiencing the self—when I lack the inner sense of being
connected to God or being part of the Tao—then a wound exists that I
experience as a gnawing, pervasive, persisting insecurity.*

*A person thus wounded seeks novelty, excitement, power, or prestige
to compensate for lack of joy or inner peace. Chronic anger and depression seem to hide just below the surfaces of the persona, or face presented
to the world. Again, this is a consequence of the wound, of the ego being
cut off from the Self. This wound affects the capacity to both give and
receive love. Emotionally, scarcity rather than abundance prevails, and
thus generosity, compassion, giving hope, and helping are all constricted
and joy and growth are stifled.*

*We can never fully grasp what is boundless, indefinite, and eternal.
Yet that small insight glimpsed or intuition felt—of the reality of the Tao
or God—is psychologically central to human experience. It nourishes
our spirit, heals our sense of isolated separateness, and restores our soul.*

I think Terry was drawn to the AA life because it is essentially
a spiritual life. She was too free a spirit to accept and practice
automatically every detail of any agenda or dogma, AA or otherwise. But she understood the AA assumption that the alcoholic

cannot control drinking except by total abstinence. How does the alcoholic achieve abstinence? He or she moves on to Step Two of the AA agenda: "Came to believe that a Power greater than ourselves could restore us to sanity."

Every AA meeting is sprinkled with references to "my Higher Power." To Terry, the Higher Power was a renewed faith in God as a spiritual being. To others, the AA fellowship is itself the Higher Power. To still others, it is a special "sponsor"—a concerned friend who helps to listen, guide, advise, and support the alcoholic's recovery. Some people testify to having been saved from alcoholism by an instant conversion—a redemptive outpouring of God's grace. But other successfully recovering alcoholics have had no such recognizable experience and may even find the whole concept of religious experience alien to their view of life.

What is important in Step One is to recognize one's powerlessness to overcome alcoholism simply by an individual effort to cut down on alcohol intake.

The alcoholic who denies that he or she is "powerless" will continue to drink, and sooner or later other problems appear—drunkenness, depression, anxiety, fear, insomnia, bad health, accidents, memory loss, declining productivity, marital complications, loss of employment, AIDS, unwanted pregnancies, child and spousal abuse, and just about every other malady imaginable.

Of course, all of these conditions may exist in the lives of both alcoholics and nonalcoholics. But all of them worsen and become less endurable when alcoholism is added to the mix. For the most part, alcoholism is the cause of the alcoholic's increasingly unhappy, problem-plagued life—not the result of such problems.

When well-meaning doctors attempt to treat an alcoholic's depression, anxiety, and fear without knowing the role of alcohol in that patient's life, they are taking the patient down a hopeless and disastrous road. This happened in some cases with Terry—especially in her early years of drinking and other drug use.

All the while she was in psychoanalysis in the late 1960s and early 1970s, she continued to drink, with perhaps inadequate appreciation on the part of her doctors that drinking was aggravating the problems they were trying to treat. Even today, many doctors and most medical schools do not give proper attention to alcoholism—notwithstanding that it is probably the nation's number one health problem.

More people are in the hospitals of America because of alcoholism than because of any other factor. More highway accidents, including thousands of deaths and crippling injuries, are caused by alcoholism than by any other factor. More unwanted pregnancies and instances of child abuse and spousal abuse are caused by alcoholism than by any other factor. More crime results from alcoholism than from any other factor. More job and productivity losses stem from alcoholism than from any other factor. The economic and social costs of alcoholism in America are staggering beyond belief. Alcoholism represents our costliest "unbalanced budget." The dollar cost alone of this addiction is estimated to be over $100 billion yearly.

These stark facts are ignored, denied, or defied by America's twenty million alcoholics, except for the one and a half million now in recovery. But what is even more alarming is that most of the rest of us also ignore, deny, or defy these hard facts.

When we encounter a person such as Teresa McGovern, drinking out of control, we tend to think this is *her* problem. Why doesn't she take hold of her life? Why can't she control her drinking like the rest of us? If she loves us, why does she keep getting drunk? Where is her willpower, where is her common sense? Or we may say, "Well, I can't do anything until she hits bottom and is such a physical, mental, and spiritual wreck that she will either have to get help or die."

The trouble with waiting for people to "hit bottom" is that they may do so only after they have destroyed their lives or the lives of others.

Neither doctors nor friends say to a person who has cancer, "Let's wait until the disease hits bottom and then we'll know what you must do." Neither should we do that with alcoholism. Reasonable effort should be made to suggest that the victim seek diagnosis of his or her problem and participation in the AA program, possibly including institutional care in a hospital or treatment center.

Terry followed this route many times, but she also relapsed many times. I have tried to sort out that trail of recovery and relapse in her life. There is no certain explanation of why some alcoholics relapse and others do not. I know of no other alcoholic who devoted more time and effort to recovery than Terry. If she sometimes neglected regular participation in the AA program and then relapsed, this leaves unanswered the question of why she would drift away from AA in the first place, setting herself up for yet another relapse. Perhaps at some level, Terry was incapable of really saying farewell to her old but treacherous friend—alcohol.

Perhaps it would have been easier for her to live without alcohol if the rest of her life had offered happier circumstances of challenging employment, satisfying romance, a comfortable home, and a stable family life. But in her more honest moments, Terry knew that all of these other pleasures and promises were dimmed and thwarted by her medication of choice—alcohol. And the more she pondered the terrible losses dealt to her by her alcoholic master, the more miserable her life became; hence the even greater demand for more and more alcohol to escape this alcohol-induced misery.

Regular attendance at AA meetings—several times each week—and a commitment to AA's Twelve Step Program seem to have brought about Terry's recovery periods. She worked hard on the program's agenda for many months of her life and achieved sobriety when she did. But that commitment wavered from time to time, and when that happened, relapse was always ready to strike and invariably did.

Terry told me several times that the Twelve Steps of AA would be helpful not only for alcoholics, but for everyone. She believed that the Prayer of St. Francis, incorporated into the AA program, was a universal prayer: "God grant me the serenity to accept the things I cannot change, the courage to change the things I can, and the wisdom to know the difference." She took pains to remind me that in the AA reference to God, the authors stress "God as we understood Him." This leaves open the various images people may have of a "Higher Power" beyond their own personal resources.

In Terry's case, the hardest of the Twelve Steps was the first one, "We admitted we were powerless over alcohol." This was also the most difficult for me and for other members of our family to accept. To the very end, Terry had times when she was in such emotional agony that she would in desperation convince herself that just one drink might fortify her against the pain that had deepened beyond her endurance. "Surely," she would rationalize, "after all I've learned about the treachery of alcohol, I'm not going to have more than one drink—or two or maybe three at the most! I may be powerless to resist a drink, but once I've had a drink I'll calm down and that will be the end of the agony that made me drink." Of course, she never stopped with one drink, and when she woke up with a hangover she felt defeated and ashamed—and the pain was even more agonizing.

And I was frequently caught up in the same syndrome. Why, I reasoned, can't Terry see what she's doing to her life with alcohol and simply give it up or at least keep it in check? If she knows I've just spent $20,000 to put her through another treatment program, won't that be enough to keep her sober? She loves her two little girls. Isn't that enough to keep her sober?

The answer to all these questions, of course, is NO. Terry, like other alcoholics, was "powerless over alcohol." Unless alcoholics really accept their powerlessness and get into a sobriety recovery plan or achieve abstinence in some other way, many of them will drink no matter what the cost to them and others until they die.

Once, when I asked Terry why she couldn't just resolve to stop drinking, she said: "Dad, recall the most powerful sexual urge you ever experienced, multiply it by ten, and then ask yourself if you could have really committed yourself to a life without any more sex no matter what the circumstances. That will give you at least a vague idea of what alcoholics feel about giving up the only real relief from the agony in their lives."

AS I HAVE traced Terry's life and reflected on what I would do differently with the benefit of hindsight, several thoughts have emerged. I would make a greater effort to share in her life and development from the beginning. I would watch over her more carefully—especially in the adolescent, high school years. I would, if I detected signs of alcoholism, inform myself thoroughly about this disease and do everything in my power to get her into a sound recovery program as quickly as possible.

In Terry's case, once the disease had fastened on to her, I would stay in close communication with her, expressing my love and concern for her at all times. I would call her every few days in a nonjudgmental manner, just to let her know I shared and understood her pain.

I regret more than I can describe the decision Eleanor and I made under professional counsel to distance ourselves from Terry in what proved to be the last six months of her life. No matter how good the intentions or great the wisdom of the counselor, this was not the right course. Terry had become so ill as the disease took its deadly toll in her final months that she needed all the attention, concern, love, and intelligent action we could have brought to bear. She should have been confined to long-term care with no opportunity to leave until she was in recovery. This method might not have worked. But we will never know that, because at the end, when she was the most helpless, it wasn't tried. It wasn't tried because we were not aware of how her disease had accelerated so rapidly in the last months.

But if I could recapture Terry's life, I would never again distance myself from her no matter how many times I had tried and failed to help her. Better to keep trying and failing than to back away and not know what is going on. If she had died despite my best efforts and my close involvement with her life up to the end, at least she would have died with my arms around her, and she would have heard me say one more time: "I love you, Terry."

Terry's inability to sustain sobriety despite her many valiant efforts has given me a new appreciation and admiration for those who have found a way to remain sober. I salute every alcoholic who day by day makes the effort and sacrifice that sobriety demands. The families and friends who have helped an alcoholic find and maintain recovery also have my highest admiration.

BUT I WANT to return to an earlier question I have struggled with throughout the writing of this book: *Why, in view of her insights and experience with both alcoholism and the satisfactions of sobriety, did Terry invariably relapse into drinking again and again?* I do not know for certain the answer to that question.

Ironically, an interview I did for *People* magazine following Terry's death inspired a research psychologist at Clemson University, Corinne Gerwe, to produce a two-hundred-page manuscript examining this maddening phenomenon of chronic relapse. After years of treating alcoholics and studying the biological, psychological, and medical findings of a wide range of authorities, Ms. Gerwe accepts the idea that alcoholism has a physiological base that contributes to the patient's emotional woes. She agrees that psychiatric counseling that ignores alcoholic intake is flawed. But she is also convinced that while unresolved emotional conflicts or traumas are not ordinarily the primary cause of alcoholism, they create behavior response patterns that can sabotage sobriety.

I am unqualified to offer a professional conclusion on this and other similar experiments, but I believe that we need more research and experimentation on matters of this kind as a possible answer to chronic relapses. Promising research focused on alcoholism and medical antidotes is now going forward at a number of institutions, including the National Institutes of Health. Recently the Food and Drug Administration approved the drug naltrexone after a decade of research on the biological roots of alcoholism. This drug seemingly reduces the craving for alcohol. Naltrexone has generally been well tolerated by patients and seems to have few side effects. Another drug, nalmefene, might prove to be even more suitable in that it carries less risk of liver toxicity.

The serotonin reuptate inhibitors are most commonly used to treat anxiety and depression, but it may also reduce the craving for alcohol. Two NIH researchers, Raye Z. Litten and John P. Allen, have concluded that "alcoholics with early onset drinking are deficient in serotonin" and "in general alcoholics with positive family history [of alcohol abuse] begin problematic drinking earlier than do their nonfamilial peers and are more likely to suffer collateral cognitive and emotional problems."

Acamprosate is still another promising drug that appears to increase abstinence.

Tiapride is a drug that seemingly reduces dependence on alcohol. Use of this drug in controlled tests has lowered the intake of alcohol by 60 percent and has increased the days of abstinence by 53 percent. The use of this drug has also resulted in improvements in self-esteem.

In addition to naltrexone, Antabuse (a brand of disulfiram) has been approved by the Food and Drug Administration. This drug has been available for the past fifty years. Its results have been mixed. The strategy of Antabuse is to create a chemical condition in the body that produces an unpleasant physical reaction—sometimes extreme nausea—when alcohol is ingested.

Terry, and many other alcoholics, have experienced depression and anxiety along with their alcoholism. The drug desipramine has been effective in countering the collateral depression of many alcoholics. Still another drug, buspirone, has reduced both the craving for alcohol and the accompanying depression and anxiety.

For the past quarter century, benzodiazepine has been used to treat the symptoms of withdrawal from alcohol. This drug tends to reduce such withdrawal symptoms as anxiety, tremors, and insomnia. It may, however, have a depressing effect on the central nervous system.

All these drugs and others, yet to be developed, cry out for more research and experimentation to determine and improve their results. I believe that research is the most promising effort in combating alcoholism and its frequent companions—depression and anxiety. Dollar for dollar, hour for hour, research is probably the most hopeful ingredient in the effort to overcome alcoholism.

How I wish that the coming breakthrough in medications, procedures, and other scientific measures to prevent or contain alcoholism had been achieved before this awful disease killed Terry. It is too late to save my daughter, but I dedicate my remaining years to advocating more research to conquer this treacherous killer.

Canceling the production of one B-2 bomber and one Seawolf submarine would free up several billion dollars that if diverted to alcohol research and treatment would contribute far more to the defense and security of the American people.

We also need to know and share, more than we do, the impact of alcoholism on the family and associates of the alcoholic. Our family probably made every mistake possible in reacting to Terry's disease—including not recognizing it as a disease for a long time. We also did some things right, and we learned a few things from our mistakes.

Alcoholism is indeed a family disease. It is a family disease in that it tends to run in some family trees more than others. It is a family disease also in that the alcoholic's disease will over time affect mental, emotional, financial, and lifestyle factors relating to the rest of the family. In a sense, the alcoholic's disease erupts in ways that threaten the entire family's health and well-being.

In our family, Terry's younger brother, Steve, has battled alcoholism since he was a teenager. Other members of the family have narrowly escaped it. There seems to be a genetic vulnerability to addiction in the McGovern clan. My paternal grandfather, Thomas McGovern, was said to be a "drinking man." My brother, Lawrence, long suffered from alcoholism before achieving a successful recovery.

In Eleanor's family, there seems to have been no alcoholism, but her maternal grandfather suffered from depression, as did one of her aunts. A favorite uncle committed suicide while in clinical depression, and, as I have mentioned, Eleanor herself has battled the hell of depression.

All of these apparent genetic factors doubtless gave Terry a vulnerability to both addiction and depression the day she was born.

The other side of the family disease is the suffering of the non-alcoholics as they are caught up in the alcoholic's behavior—a behavior that produces disappointment, shattered expectations, anxiety, and anguish.

I spent many restless nights worrying about Teresa. If alcoholism produces insomnia for its victims, the family also battles this sleeplessness. I dreaded the late-night or early-morning telephone call lest it bring some new note of trouble and disappointment. I became obsessed with Terry's impact on our family gatherings, her children, her siblings, her employers, and her landlords, and her constant encounters with the police, emergency rooms, and treatment and detox centers.

It pained me to feel the resentment of my other children, who understandably wondered if a parent so obsessed with one child had any time or concern left for them. Sometimes I tried to pull away from Terry even when she may have most needed me because I wanted the others to see that I wasn't totally absorbed in their sister.

I recall with considerable pain that Terry begged me to participate more actively in Al-Anon—the offshoot of AA designed for families and friends of alcoholism. Usually, I excused my not doing so because of my heavy schedule. Ironically, I have devoted a hundred times more study, inquiry, and investigation to alcoholism in the months since Terry's death than in the forty-five years of her life. I have pressed Eleanor to recall insights she may have gained from hundreds of hours of concerned conversation with Terry over many years. I have pursued her brother and sisters, her many friends and associates, her little daughters, her ex-mates, her therapists, and her fellow alcoholics in an effort to understand this very special daughter. Why did it take her death to trigger this search for understanding of the affliction that scarred her troubled life and in the end brought her to an untimely grave? Why couldn't I have gained my present knowledge and understanding of my daughter and her disease in time to have helped her more effectively than I did?

I can't give satisfying answers to these questions. What I can tell you is that the sorrow of losing one of your children is almost unbearable. It is sad beyond any measure that I had imagined.

If you have a troubled or addicted daughter or son, do not ever imagine that you or your child might be better off if death were to steal her or him away. Death is devastating and final and agonizing for a parent. There is no way you can avoid a full measure of painful regrets and might-have-beens.

Your friends and counselors will tell you: "Don't blame yourself. It's not your fault—you did the best you could." This advice is well meant and may even be true. It doesn't help much. You'll be sad, and you will hurt when you lie down to sleep, when you awake in the night, when you rise in the morning, when you go to a beach where she swam, when you drive past her school, when you hear her children laughing, when you see a Christmas tree, or whenever you recall her dancing eyes, her lingering embrace, her glorious smile when she saw you at the airport—or her anguish when she fell from intoxication. I'm especially sad on June 10—her birthday—and on December 13, when she died in the snow.

But you will also discover that life goes on. Her children fill the vacancy with play and school and laughter and tears, just as she once did. The memories of her life take on a comforting quality. The visits to her grave become less agonizing. The lives of your other children and their children help to fill your life with a thousand different joys, concerns, and satisfactions.

Eleanor and I glory in our good fortune to be the parents of four daughters and a son and the grandparents of nine grandchildren. Each of them fascinates and enriches us with his or her uniqueness, imagination, creativity, and wit. Each of them has contributed something of value to this story about the only one in the family who has died. I can't capture or quote all of their thoughts, but let me reproduce a few paragraphs our oldest daughter, Ann, wrote upon reading a draft of this book.

I believe her life, as painful as it often was for her to live and for those who loved her to witness, has much to teach us. She, Teresa Jane McGovern, in her own unique subjective life, had much to say that revealed eternal truths that are at the heart of religions and mythology.

Some of the truths her life revealed are:

1. Treat other living creatures as you would like to be treated: she knew what it is to feel vulnerable, incomplete, afraid, unwell, fragile; so she saw the pain of others and reached out to offer comfort, solace, hope. One of her gifts was that she did touch people—she rarely "preached" or intellectualized about life. She did not live by slogans or clichés. You know there was something special about Terry—most people who came into contact with her knew that about her. That quality was active in her life throughout the last day of her life even as her mind was "blacked out" and her body once again consumed by alcohol. In other words, something in Terry (call it soul, heart, love) transcended all else. I think the juxtaposition of her last days/hours as they're recorded in medical and police reports with her compassion for the elderly crippled person outside the licensing bureau is profound. It is not her beliefs or anyone else's beliefs alone that matter but how we treat the people whom we encounter in this life. She engaged people throughout her life even up to her last moments.

2. I think we honor Terry's life and memory when we allow her to speak for herself. Her truth as it's revealed in her journals, her interactions with others and how people felt about her, are worthy and need no interpretation by others. She is eloquent and profound in her own words.

3. Another truth that Terry's life reveals is how difficult it is to simply love one another. As often as not, Terry was able to love and to express love, with her fellow human be-

ings wherever she met them. She found it difficult, even impossible, sometimes to love herself.

We, all of us, fell short of simply loving her. I think we listened to the dogma or advice of others—with the best of intentions and with our limited understanding. But as I
remember Terry and read her words, what she needed and
wanted was simply love and acceptance; shelter and safety.

I wish I had held her more; had accepted her more; had
judged and criticized her less; tried to understand her less
and loved her more just as she was. The truth that I was coming to know in the months before she died was that she was
no threat to me—she was a fragile, suffering younger sister,
and I had much more love than I ever showed her. I, like you,
and all of us, must accept our own human shortcomings and
limits. It is not given to us to have one minute back with
Terry—we have her in memory and memory is a living facet
of life. We also have her "charge" to us to love more fully
those with whom we still do have time—her daughters are
with us and there are "thousands" of "Terrys" in the world
who need our compassion and our help. We honor Terry
when we speak kindly; when we withhold judgment; when
we accept the least among us; when we offer solace and
healing.

There is, I believe, no answer to the whys of Terry's life and
death, but there is much we can learn from her.

I believe Terry was touched by grace—that God was merciful that night last December. I know an angel was waiting
for Terry—had been waiting for her all her life. I have no
doubt Terry's soul returned for a few minutes to me the night
after I'd learned she died. She gave a great healing gift to
me—answered prayer if you will. She told me *she* was filled;
she was loved and loving; she was free. She was formless, but
some essential part of Terry is in the world and always will be;
she is home and she is all that she wanted her *self* to be and
more.

After her 1993 temporary recovery experience at Ashley House in Maryland, Terry wrote in her journal, "I want to write a book—autobiographical and recovery-focused—the quiet but persistent murmurings of spiritual longing that finally took hold at Ashley: *Angels and Miracles in My Life.*"

The Fates did not allow Terry to write that book. This is too bad, because she was a talented, imaginative writer with a drama that needed to be told as only she could have.

This is my limited but loving quest to tell Terry's untold story. Already it has enabled me to hear the first whispering of her immortality.

"Bancroft's advice to historians: present your subject in his own terms, judge him in yours. Actually, I'd just as soon leave out the judgment entirely. I don't feel at ease judging people."

—WALLACE STEGNER,
Angle of Repose

Terry and me at her last birthday party, June 10, 1994, in Milwaukee.

EPILOGUE

T erry's funeral was held on Saturday morning, December 17, 1994, at Washington's beautiful and historic Foundry United Methodist Church, just a few blocks from the White House. It was a tearful but inspiring experience. Dr. Philip Wogoman, our minister—a former professor of ethics—spoke, as always, with compassionate insight. Eileen Guenther, the Foundry organist, and Susan Bender, a soprano soloist in the church choir, opened the service with Handel's beautiful aria from the *Messiah*, "He Shall Feed His Flocks." As Susan later sang "Ave Maria"—a favorite of Terry's—Colleen and Marian led a heart-stirring procession of our grandchildren, each placing a white rose on Terry's oak casket, which had previously been covered with red roses.

Between Susan's beautiful solos, Terry's college roommate and friend Nikki Abourezk poured her soul into singing the old spiritual "A Closer Walk with Thee"—another Terry favorite. Our four older grandsons—Tim, Kevin, Matt, and Sam—read biblical passages from Ecclesiastes, Isaiah, and Matthew that we thought reflected Terry's philosophy.

Several hundred people, including many of my former staffers in the Senate and from the 1972 presidential campaign, came to the funeral. Our family was pleased to see Ethel Kennedy there with her longtime friend Elizabeth Stevens. I thought not only of Ethel's loss of her husband, Robert, to an assassin's bullet, but also of the subsequent death of her son David from a drug overdose. David, a friend of our youngest daughter, Mary, visited our house numerous times.

Jeff Smith and Jim McGovern (no relation), two treasured friends and former staff members, served as pallbearers, along with our four older grandsons and two nephews, Robert Pennington and Scotty Peterson.

Terry's friend Don Berlin, who was in treatment with her, told the mourners that Terry had saved his life by pushing him back into treatment and recovery as he was about to flee to Thailand.

I reproduce here the stirring eulogies of Bob Shrum, our close family friend who has helped me in the drafting of speeches for many years, and Hobart Rowen, the longtime economics writer for *The Washington Post*, recently deceased, whose son Jim is married to our daughter Sue.

Remarks of Robert Shrum at Terry's funeral:

> Over the years, George McGovern has asked me to write a number of things. He has given me the privilege of working with him. He and Eleanor have given me one of the enduring friendships of my life.
>
> Now today, like everyone in this church, I want to cry out that something this bad should not have happened to these good people. Like many of you, I knew Terry best in the 1972 campaign. She was one of the brightest stars of an enterprise that made many stars, including the man who is now President of the United States. She gave hundreds of speeches in those intense months, spoke to thousands of people, led a caravan across the South known as the Grasshopper Special.

She had her father's passion on great issues and her mother's gentleness. People liked her, and were instinctively drawn to her. She went out of her way to learn the names of so many of the young legion who joined in the crusade. I will never forget how bravely she smiled through the tears on election night, and reached out to touch the hands of others.

The campaign had been a happy time—but as we grow up, we all learn that the world also has its hurts and sometimes breaks our hearts. That election night was one of the nights when a lot of us grew up. That night, and in many ways since then, George and Eleanor have shown such amazing grace.

But I know it is one of their greatest sadnesses that despite everything they tried, they could not heal Terry—who, for all her gifts, was painfully vulnerable. Susan and Jim, Ann and Frank, Steve, Mary and Fabian, Ray and their children and her nieces and nephews—they all tried to help. And it should be stated Terry fought back again and again; she fought back hard. I last saw her a year ago at the fiftieth wedding anniversary celebration for her parents. To those of us who were there, she was joyous, full of life and hope—and most of all, of love for her children.

To George and Eleanor, I want to say for so many of us, here and elsewhere, that we know what you meant to Terry—because you brought us, too, into your family. A whole cadre of us who, for more than twenty years, no matter where we are, have felt close to you. We, too, are your sons and daughters. We, too, are Terry's brothers and sisters.

So today I think of Terry McGovern standing there on the Grasshopper Special, a vibrant young woman speaking out for peace and justice all over this land. She was full of decency and high ideals.

She was a "McGovernick," and she was fiercely proud of it.

• • •

Remarks of Hobart Rowen at Terry's funeral.

The Rowens and McGoverns joined forces twenty-seven years ago in 1967, when my son Jim Rowen and Susan McGovern were married. Over that long span of years, we have shared many joys as friends and relatives, notably two wonderful grandchildren, Matt McGovern-Rowen and Sam McGovern-Rowen. Alice and I and George and Eleanor celebrated golden wedding anniversaries barely a year apart. So there are many things, including a reluctance to discard the Big L in politics, that bring us together. I think our relationships have become increasingly close with the mellowing of years. But there is one special Rowen-McGovern tie that only a few of you know about, the one that grew between Terry and me. Terry, despite her illness and multiple problems, was a most compassionate person. About a year ago, when Terry learned from Jim that I was not doing particularly well in fighting prostate cancer, she phoned me to offer hope. This was a surprise; Terry and I had not been particularly close; our paths had not crossed often in recent years. But there was Terry at the other end of the phone counseling me not to despair. "Don't give up," she said. "Be optimistic. The mind can do wonderful things for the body. Have faith." She even called back with a reading list of mind-over-body books, like Deepak Chopra's.

In turn, I tried to turn Terry's words of faith back onto herself, to convince her that she too could solve her problems. At that point, she was convinced she could make it. Over shared tears, our affirmation of confidence was an expression of belief in a higher force.

The point of my story is that Terry, who in the end wasn't able to help herself, was able to help others. She helped me regain my equilibrium. Like Don Berlin, I too recovered a gift from Terry. I am learning to be grateful for every day. That's something I owe in part to Terry McGovern, something I will always remember.

• • •

AFTER THE FUNERAL, only the family went to Rock Creek Cemetery—Washington's beautiful and oldest cemetery, where Terry was buried next to a large Celtic cross dedicated to the original benefactor of the cemetery, John Bradford, who in 1719 gave the Episcopal Church the hundred acres of land that make up the cemetery. The nearby Episcopal church, established in 1712, is the oldest church in the nation's capital. Terry's grave is located in what Eleanor and I regard as the most desirable site in the cemetery. Why no one had chosen it in the past two centuries, I cannot imagine.

The grave marker reads:

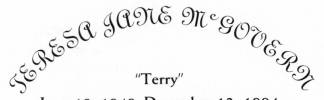

"Terry"
June 10, 1949–December 13, 1994
Precious daughter of
George and Eleanor McGovern

I DOUBT THAT any parent ever fully recovers from the recurring sadness involved in the death of a child. But my family and I have found some ways to ease the pain of losing Terry. A wonderful memorial service to Terry in Madison a month after her death organized by our daughter Sue and her husband, Jim Rowen, gave Terry's Wisconsin friends and our family an opportunity to express informally our memories of Terry—including the fun and laughter. On Terry's first birthday after her death, June 10, 1995, we gathered in Madison again, this time to dedicate a simple but beautiful shrine in Terry's memory outside the Tellurian

Center, where she spent so many of her last days. Her friend Don Berlin largely financed this project—two lovely Black Hills spruce trees, a handsome hardwood bench, and a lighted marble marker. On this same day we dedicated a marking post at the place behind the Lakeside Print Shop where Terry died. Norman Stockwell, the owner of the shop, who discovered Terry's body in the snow, has surrounded the marker with a small garden, which he lovingly maintains.

Writing this book and speaking out on alcoholism have helped to ease the pain of losing Terry. Supporting the building of Tellurian's new Teresa McGovern Treatment Center in Madison has been another healing effort. The creation of the Teresa Educational Trust for the education of Terry's two daughters, Marian and Colleen, is another.

Potentially the most helpful action we have taken is the establishment of the McGovern Family Foundation to receive and disburse funds primarily for research on alcoholism, with special emphasis on the problem of relapse, which took Terry's life and continues to sabotage the recovery of so many alcoholics. Tax-deductible contributions may be sent to:

The McGovern Family Foundation
P.O. Box 33393
Washington, D.C. 20033

Contributions to this research effort will transform Terry's death into a means of saving the lives of others.

ACKNOWLEDGMENTS

I thank the editors of *People* magazine for pushing me into an early article on Terry's life-and-death struggle with alcoholism. I'm also especially grateful to Walter Anderson, the editor of *Parade* magazine, for opening the huge circulation of his remarkable journal to this story. The producers of ABC's *PrimeTime Live* effectively dramatized Terry's tragedy, while CNN's *Larry King Live* and Judy Woodruff, ABC's Julie London, and others broadened public understanding of the issues involved and prompted me to think about the need for this book.

I especially want to thank a talented young journalist of *The Washington Post*, Laura Blumenfeld, whose brilliant and sensitive account of Terry's life and death is a superb journalistic achievement. Laura's writing and conversations have helped to inspire these chapters, which she has read critically and helpfully.

I thank Esther Newburg, my agent, who believed this book should be written and who worked out arrangements with one of the nation's great publishers—and then closely followed the progress of the manuscript.

I especially want to thank my superb editor and publisher at Villard Books of Random House, David Rosenthal. He has, from beginning to end, advised, criticized, inspired, and pushed me to do my best in creating and completing this work. I'm deeply indebted to David for improving my own efforts.

I'm also indebted to David's assistants, Tad Floridis and the painstaking Jennifer Webb. Villard's associate publisher, Annik LaFarge; Dan Rembert, who designed the book jacket; Adam Rothberg, who promoted the book; and associate copy chief Beth Pearson have been most helpful.

I thank Terry's many friends and associates for speaking to me candidly about their experiences and insights.

Thanks also to Jeff Jay, a specialist on alcoholism; Professor Lorraine Duke of Marshall University; Professor Steve Ambrose of the University of New Orleans; Professor Tom Knock of Southern Methodist University; my longtime friend Bob Shrum; and Anne Joyce, my colleague at the Middle East Policy Council, for reading all or portions of the manuscript critically and giving me the benefit of their thoughts.

I am most grateful to my assistant Susan Straight, who tirelessly and repeatedly transformed my not always legible handwriting into a carefully typed text. She has helped me rework and improve numerous drafts of the book.

Finally, I thank my dear wife, Eleanor, and our children—Ann, Sue, Steve, and Mary—for their love and sharing during the days and nights since December 13, 1994. This book is my personal testament, but it could not have been written, nor could I have withstood the loss of Terry, without the generous participation and love of my wife, children, and grandchildren.

ABOUT THE AUTHOR

GEORGE MCGOVERN is a former United States Senator, and he was the Democratic party candidate for President in 1972. He currently heads the Middle East Policy Council in Washington, D.C., where he lives.